RUDOLF S
The Man and His Vision

Other Aquarian books by Colin Wilson
ALEISTER CROWLEY: The Nature of the Beast
G. I. GURDJIEFF: The War Against Sleep
C. G. JUNG: Lord of the Underworld

RUDOLF
STEINER
The Man and His Vision

An Introduction to the Life and Ideas
of the Founder of Anthroposophy

by

Colin Wilson

THE AQUARIAN PRESS

First published 1985

© COLIN WILSON 1985

British Library Cataloguing in Publication Data

Wilson, Colin, 1931-
Rudolf Steiner: the man and his vision.
1. Steiner, Rudolf
I. Title
193   BP595.S895

ISBN 0-85030-398-2

The Aquarian Press is part of the Thorsons Publishing Group, Wellingborough, Northamptonshire NN8 2RQ, England

Printed in Great Britain by Woolnough Bookbinding Limited, Irthlingborough, Northamptonshire

3 5 7 9 10 8 6 4

Contents

Acknowledgements

I WISH to express my gratitude to members of the Anthroposophical Society in Great Britain and particularly to Mrs E. Lloyd, who used to run the Steiner Bookshop at Museum Street, London WC1. I also wish to thank John Bowyer for providing me with material and for many helpful suggestions and Eileen Hutchins for her interesting comment on the problem of Steiner's 'vision' of King Arthur at Tintagel.

It need hardly be emphasized that the members of the Anthroposophical Society who have offered their help should be in no way held responsible for the views expressed in the present book.

I also wish to thank the London Library, and in particular Christopher Hurley, for valuable help.

I also owe a debt of enormous gratitude to Dan Lloyd, who sent me invaluable photostat material of lectures by Steiner not published in English.

One

The Door to the Inner Universe

OF ALL the important thinkers of the twentieth century, Rudolf Steiner is perhaps the most difficult to come to grips with. For the unprepared reader, his work presents a series of daunting obstacles. To begin with, there is the style, which is formidably abstract, and as unappetizing as dry toast. But a determined reader could learn to put up with that. The real problem lies in the content, which is often so outlandish and bizarre that the reader suspects either a hoax or a barefaced confidence trick. Books like *Cosmic Memory*, with its account of Atlantis and Lemuria, seem to belong on the same shelf as titles like *Our Hollow Earth*, or *My Trip to Venus in a Flying Saucer*. The resulting sense of frustration is likely to cause even the most open-minded reader to give up in disgust.

This was, I must admit, my own experience when the publisher of the present volume approached me in the mid-1970s and asked me to write a book on Steiner. I accepted because I had always found Steiner an interesting figure. I first came upon his name in my early teens; it was in a remarkable book called *God Is My Adventure*, by Rom Landau. Landau begins his account by describing the experience of a certain Baron V—, a German officer with whom the author became acquainted during his student days in Warsaw. The Baron was a member of a flying corps on the western front in the First World War, and he developed a disturbing psychic faculty: the ability to foretell which of his comrades would be killed when they flew out on a mission. This gift of prophecy threatened to wreck his health, so when he was advised to go and see a certain Dr Rudolf Steiner, he seized the idea with relief. Dr Steiner proved to be a quiet man with deep-set eyes, and he advised the baron to practise certain simple mental disciplines. These had the desired effect, and the unnerving gift vanished.

Landau's account made it clear that Steiner was no charlatan messiah; whenever people met this calm, serious man and heard him speak quietly and sensibly about the 'spirit world', they felt he was speaking from direct experience.

Over the years, I had picked up many copies of Steiner's books in second-hand shops. I had dipped into them, but found the style off-putting. I promised myself that one of these days I would settle down to a systematic study of Steiner's ideas, and the publisher's offer seemed to be the opportunity I had been waiting for. So I accepted, and blew the dust off the dozen or so volumes of Steiner on my bookshelves.

There seems to be a general agreement that *An Outline of Occult Science* is Steiner's most important book, so I started with that. It begins by acknowledging that 'occult science' is regarded with suspicion by many people, a danger to weak minds. It goes on: 'All occult science is born from two thoughts . . . first, that behind the visible world there is another, the invisible world, which is hidden from the senses, and from thought that is fettered by the senses; secondly, that it is possible for man to penetrate into that unseen world by developing certain faculties dormant within him.'

So far, so good. After another ten pages of introductory matter, Steiner launches into a chapter on the nature of man. And its opening paragraph proceeds to repeat what he has already said more briefly and effectively:

Considering man in the light of occult science, we are at once reminded of its general characteristics. It rests upon the recognition of a hidden something behind that which is manifest to the outer senses and to the intellect brought to bear upon their perceptions. These senses and this intellect can apprehend only a part of all that which occult science unveils as the total human entity, and this part is what occult science calls the physical body . . . .

I was already becoming irritated by this repetition of the words 'occult science', and by what sounds like an attempt to impress by sheer wordiness ('this part is what occult science calls the physical body'; why not just: 'i.e. the body'). He goes on:

> In order to throw light on its conception of this body, occult science at first directs attention to a phenomenon which confronts all observers of life like a great riddle—the phenomenon of death—and in connection with it occult science points to so-called inanimate nature, the mineral kingdom. We are thus referred to facts which it devolves on occult science to explain, and to which an important part of this work must be devoted.

Gurdjieff's followers suspect that he wrote certain works—like *Beelzebub's Tales to his Grandson*—in a deliberately complicated style, to force the reader to make enormous mental efforts. I wondered at first whether this was Steiner's intention: to weed out the lazy. But further reading makes it clear that this is Steiner's natural way of expressing himself.

I persevered for another week, reading various other works by Steiner: *Theosophy, Knowledge of Higher Worlds, Christianity as a Mystical Fact*, and finally gave up. I wrote a regretful line to the publisher telling him that, with the best will in the world, I just couldn't go through with it. In large doses, Steiner simply infuriated me. The publisher was perfectly amiable about it. He approached that brilliant cultural historian of the 'occult underground', James Webb, who agreed to write the book.

Alas, Webb began to show signs of mental instability in 1979, and on 8 May 1980, he committed suicide with a rifle. Webb and I had been in correspondence over the years, and I was saddened by his death. I also found myself wondering whether his attempt to digest hundreds of yards of Steiner's woolly prose had anything to do with his suicide. Webb's own drily ironic account of Steiner in his book *The Occult Establishment* (1976)—in a chapter entitled 'Ginungagapp'—makes it clear that his book would have been written from the viewpoint of an 'unbeliever'.

But circumstances were to draw me back to Steiner. In 1982, I started making plans to write a history of psychometry—the strange ability of certain people to hold an object in their hands and 'see' its history. This is by no means as absurd as it sounds. The word was invented by J. Rhodes Buchanan, an American professor of medicine, in the mid-nineteenth century. A bishop named Polk happened to tell Buchanan that he could distinguish brass in the dark by touching it with his fingertips—it caused a peculiar brassy taste in his mouth. Buchanan noted this as a medical curiosity, and discovered that many of his students possessed the same faculty. They were able, for example, to identify various chemicals wrapped in thick brown paper packages, merely by touching them. But the strangest thing of all was when Buchanan discovered a man who could hold a sealed letter in his hand, and 'sense' the mood and the background of the person who wrote it.

Buchanan's discoveries were taken up by a professor of geology named William Denton; he discovered that 'sensitives' could hold a geological specimen—a meteorite, a piece of dinosaur bone, a fragment of tile from a Roman villa—and see visions of its history. Denton, like Buchanan, was convinced that this was a perfectly normal human faculty, merely waiting to be developed, a kind of 'telescope into the past'. He had no doubt that it would revolutionize the science of history, as historians trained themselves to hold some relic from a battlefield or death chamber, and to witness scenes from the past as if watching some ancient film material from the archives.

Regrettably, the birth of 'spiritualism' in the 1850s led to bitter controversies, and caused scientists to dismiss anything that sounded even vaguely 'occult'. Buchanan and Denton were tarred with the same brush as Madame Blavatsky and Daniel Dunglas Home (Browning's 'Mr Sludge the Medium') and their attempt to create a new science was forgotten.

That remarkable and irrepressible lady Madame Blavatsky also claimed to possess a certain power of psychometry. In her two major works, *Isis Unveiled* and *The Secret Doctrine*, she states that the universe is permeated by a kind of psychic ether called *Akasa*—telepathy and clairvoyance are 'waves' in this ether. *Akasa* also records everything that has ever happened, like some incredible combination of film camera and gramophone record, and the 'Akasic (or Akashic) records' can be 'played back' by psychics and clairvoyants. Madame

Blavatsky wrote a great deal about the history of Atlantis, Lemuria and other 'ancient civilizations', claiming to have acquired her knowledge direct from the Akasic records. And in his book *Cosmic Memory*, Steiner makes much the same claim.

All this has done Steiner's reputation no good. In *The Occult Establishment*, James Webb represents him as a kind of gifted dabbler with the mind of a jackdaw. 'Steiner's ideas form less of a "system" than an accumulation of sometimes disconnected items. Thus from Theosophy he took the ideas of *karma* and reincarnation; from his mystical studies and possibly the O.T.O [a dubious magical order], a personal "Rosicrucianism". He discovered an entirely new idiosyncratic and personal interpretation of Christianity, and somehow contrived a seeming coherence with these teachings for theories of the social and artistic life of man.' In other words, Steiner was an intellectual opportunist who patched together his own religious system from attractive bits and pieces of other people's ideas. And when he goes on to talk about the 'gaggle of adoring women' who caused the break-up of Steiner's first marriage, and a tale (told by Steiner's stepdaughter) of how her mother found Steiner in bed with one of his disciples, it is not difficult to read between the lines to his view of Steiner as a pious fraud.

In order to write the section of my *Psychic Detectives* that dealt with 'The Akasic records', I had to renew my acquaintance with Rudolf Steiner. I read the biography by Johannes Hemleben, and set out to trace the development of his ideas from his early days in the Goethe Archive, where he edited Goethe's scientific writings. This led me to look at early works like *The Philosophy of Freedom* and *Goethe's World View*. Rather to my surprise, I discovered that Steiner was a philosopher and cultural historian of considerable brilliance. There was not the slightest flavour of the bogus in these works—on the contrary, they give the impression of a man who is totally fascinated by the history of ideas, and who tries to say what he has to say as simply and clearly as he can. The rather abstract quality of his style is due to complete lack of artifice; he is not out to impress—either with beauty of style, or with an obscurity that might be mistaken for profundity. A reference

to Goethe, the man Steiner admired above everyone, led me
to look up the passage in question, and it suddenly struck me
that this is the key to Steiner's style. To modern ears, Goethe's
prose sounds disagreeably stiff and stilted—even in novels
like *Wilhelm Meister* and *Elective Affinities*. The *Conversations
with Eckermann* indicate that he even talked like that: 'Religion
stands in the same relation to art as any other of the higher
interests of life. It is merely to be looked upon as a material,
with similar claims to any other vital material. Faith and want
of faith are not the organs with which a work of art is to be
apprehended. On the contrary, human powers and capacities
of a totally different character are required. . . .' The thought is
perfectly clear, but it is hard to imagine a modern sage, even if
he happened to be a university professor, expressing himself
in this rather abstract manner. I believe that, after years of
working in the Goethe Archive in Weimar, Goethe's prose
style simply became second nature to Steiner.

I also found myself in deep sympathy with what Steiner is
trying to do in these early works. Like the young H. G. Wells
at about the same time, he was fascinated by science and the
scientific method. Yet he was revolted by the materialistic
world-picture of modern science. He wanted to show that it
simply wouldn't hold water—that total material *fails to account*
for the complexities of the universe and of human existence.
But he was not content with denouncing it on vaguely poetic
or artistic grounds. He wanted to get an intellectual crowbar
underneath it and overturn it from the foundations. Madame
Blavatsky also spends a great deal of time in *Isis Unveiled*
attacking modern science; but as a spiritualist and an 'occultist'
she never stood the slightest chance of convincing a single
scientist. Steiner argues as someone with an immense grasp of
modern science and philosophy, and the result is impressive.
If Steiner had died before he took the leap into 'occultism', he
would now be classified with Bergson, Whitehead, Samuel
Alexander, Hans Driesch, Edmund Husserl, Maurice Merleau-
Ponty, and Karl Popper as a philosopher who wanted to
demonstrate that scientific materialism is too *narrow*.

After reading these books I felt stricken with guilt—like a
man who has condemned someone as a crook and then
discovered he is rigidly honest. It was possible, of course, that

Steiner had 'sold out' after about 1900, and decided to settle for the rewards of a religious messiah; but on the evidence of his early writing, that seemed unlikely. Self-deception comes hard to men of Steiner's type.

Because I had become so fascinated by the development of Steiner's ideas, the section I wrote about him in my history of psychometry—*The Psychic Detectives*—was far too long. When it came to a question of cutting the book by a few thousand words, these pages on Steiner's philosophical ideas seemed an obvious candidate. But removing them caused so much regret that I thereupon decided to use them as the foundation of a book on Steiner. I wrote to the publisher and asked him if he was still interested; fortunately, he was. So once again, I took a deep breath and plunged into the works of Steiner.

This time I decided to begin with the autobiography he had written two years before his death. It was a happy decision. Pupils had asked Steiner to write something about his intellectual development, and he did this in a series of articles that were published in the 'house magazine' of the Anthroposophical Society, *The Goetheanum*. Since he was writing for students and disciples, and not for the general public, Steiner obviously felt that he could write about anything that interested him, and pause for lengthy ruminations whenever he felt inclined. After four hundred pages, he had only brought the narrative as far as the year 1907, and at that point he died, worn out by the burdens of a messiah with too many disciples. (There must have been times when he felt like a cake divided into crumbs.) The result is a marvellously detailed account of his early development which answers every major question. It also leaves no possible doubt that there was any fundamental change of direction in Steiner's life. By the early 1890s—by which time he was in his early thirties—Steiner had already developed all the insights that were to form the basis of his 'occult science'. W. B. Yeats once said that when he went to London, he was like an old brass cannon primed to explode. The same is true of Steiner when he went to Berlin in 1897. He was prepared to launch a new vision of human evolution on the world.

What then went wrong?—for there is no doubt in my mind that something *did* go wrong, leading to his early death at the age of sixty-four. (He had always been in robust health, and might have been expected, like Goethe, to live into his eighties.) I suspect that he made his first major mistake in agreeing to become the German head of the Theosophical Society, the organization founded by Madame Blavatsky. Intellectually speaking, Steiner was far more of a heavyweight than anyone in the Society. He had already formulated his basic philosophy. He had nothing whatever to gain from association with people who were regarded as occultist cranks, who believed that Madame Blavatsky was the mouth-piece of Secret Masters who lived on mountaintops in Tibet. Worse still, the Theosophists discovered a new messiah in 1909, a fourteen-year-old Hindu boy named Jiddu Krishnamurti, and announced that he was to be the next world saviour. Steiner flatly declined to accept this, and not long thereafter, severed his connection with the Theosophists. But it was too late to prevent himself being tarred with the same brush as the Theosophists. It has done Steiner's reputation no good whatever to be bracketed with Madame Blavatsky.

But there was another problem, which Steiner could not possibly have foreseen. In the nineteenth century, it was possible to be a celebrity and still have a reasonable degree of privacy. And this was not simply because, in the days before newspaper photographs, celebrities were not so easily recognized. Charles Dickens was involved in a train crash. He went to the guard and said: 'Do you know who I am?' 'Yes, sir', said the man, 'Mr Dickens.' 'Good,' said Dickens, 'then do as I tell you,' and proceeded to take charge of the rescue operation. But if the same guard had seen Dickens in the street or eating in a restaurant, he would certainly not have rushed up to him for his autograph. The change that came about in the twentieth century was largely due to new means of communication: radio, cinema, mass circulation news-papers. These have had the effect of widening the psychological gap between the 'famous man' and the man in the street. If everybody in the civilized world knows the name of Charlie Chaplin or Greta Garbo, then it is natural for most people to exaggerate their importance, to imagine them surrounded by some kind of magical aura. So the knowledge that one of these god-like figures is staying in a certain hotel is enough to cause crowds of people to stand around, hoping to catch a glimpse of the prodigy. Steiner grew to manhood in the age of Dickens, but he became a celebrity in the age of Charlie Chaplin. His biographer, Guenther Wachsmuth, mentions that, in the early days, Steiner tried to give personal help and advice to as many of his followers as possible, but that this became impossible as his following swelled. Another biographer, Albert Steffen, speaks of the queues of people waiting outside Steiner's door from morning till night, waiting to pour out their problems and ask his advice.

Steiner also suffered from another consequence of the 'celebrity mechanism': malice. When a man is regarded with admiration (or, worse still, reverence) by a large number of people, he is bound to arouse a hostility in those who feel, quite unconsciously, that they too deserve to be admired and revered. Steffen comments on the complete lack of malicious gossip among Steiner's own disciples in those early years; they felt so exalted by Steiner's teaching that malice would have been unthinkable. But this in itself would be enough to make outsiders feel that this was a rather disgusting clique, a mutual admiration society that badly needed the corrective of a little plain speaking. When Steiner decided to deliver his message to the world in the form of lectures and articles, he felt that it was his task to explain what he had learned from twenty years of study and meditation. He probably expected bafflement or lack of interest; he can hardly have anticipated the tempest of hostility that led to the burning down of the Goetheanum and attempts to beat him up in a hotel. Although Steffen says that Steiner was sustained by enormous spiritual strength, there is still a strong case to be made for the argument that he died of discouragement.

Since Steiner's death, his ideas have lived on in schools devoted to his educational theories, in farms based on his agricultural ideas, even in hospitals and clinics founded on his beliefs about the relation of the body and spirit. Yet the work that Steiner himself would have regarded as most important—what might be called his 'philosophy of spiritual activity'—has never succeeded in percolating through to the educated public. You would expect a man of fairly wide culture to know something about Jung, something about the

Maharishi, something about Buckminster Fuller and Marshall McLuhan, perhaps even something about Gurdjieff and Ouspensky. But even among intellectuals, very few would have the vaguest idea about Rudolf Steiner's philosophy.

So before embarking on a systematic exposition of his life and works, let me attempt to sketch his fundamental idea. Once this has been grasped, everything else follows. Without this key, his work is bound to appear a disconnected chaos of theories and speculations.

Steiner's starting point is the belief that 'behind' this material world, revealed by our senses, there is a supersensible or spiritual world. This sounds, of course, like the central belief of most of the great world religions, but in Steiner's case there is an important corollary. He was also convinced that, by a simple training, anybody can develop the faculty of seeing this other realm of being. He himself claimed to have achieved this ability, and he did his best to show his followers how to achieve it.

It is important not to confuse Steiner's 'supersensory perception' with clairvoyance or mediumship. Unlike Madame Blavatsky, who started her career as a spirit medium, Steiner was deeply suspicious of spiritualism. It was not that he disputed the basic facts: that there is life after death and that man can communicate with 'spirits'. But he felt that the spiritualists were wasting their time by concentrating on these phenomena. Suppose you could pick up some kind of psychic telephone and dial Albert Einstein in heaven (or wherever he is). Would it teach you about the theory of relativity, or help you to grasp his conception of space-time? Obviously not. If you want to know about these things, then you have to put a great deal of mental energy into learning about them. And when you have done that, you will, in a sense, 'know' Einstein a great deal better than if you had been allowed to speak to him. And communicating with spirits, either through a ouija board or in the seance room, will not give you the slightest conception about the realms of meaning that are hidden behind the face of material reality. This demands the development of a peculiar kind of vision, an 'inward vision'. And, according to Steiner, this inward vision is achieved in three distinct stages. The first he labels 'thought' (or imagination), the second 'inspiration', and the third 'intuition'.

This sounds harmless—and insipid—enough. But there is nothing insipid or vague about Steiner's exposition of the three stages. It is precise, detailed, and pragmatic. He never speaks with the accents of a would-be prophet trying to pull the wool over your eyes. He is more like a teacher of mathematics, doing his best to make his students follow his reasoning.

The first and most important stage of insight is thought. It is the most important because it is the bridge between our ordinary, muddled state of everyday consciousness and the states of 'higher knowledge'. I shall devote the remainder of this chapter to attempting to show exactly what Steiner means by this first stage. Once this has been grasped, the reader has passed through the doorway into the world of Steiner's own vision of human evolution.

We may start from the simple observation that human consciousness spends most of its time trapped in the physical world. According to Sartre, this is the basic truth of human existence; man is stuck in physical existence like a fly on fly paper. It is worth mentioning Sartre at this point, for his thought is in every way diametrically opposed to Steiner, and can be used as a kind of philosophical 'ground bass' against which Steiner's ideas can be measured. According to Sartre, human life is meaningless and therefore tragic. When a man feels tired—or utterly bored with some repetitive routine— he may suddenly become fully aware of this meaninglessness. He experiences the feeling 'What am I doing here?' The world suddenly looks frightening and alien. Sartre calls this sudden recognition of meaninglessness 'nausea' or 'the absurd'. (Camus borrowed the term from him.) According to Sartre, 'nausea' reveals the basic truth about human existence: that 'it is meaningless that we live and meaningless that we die'. 'Man', says Sartre, is a 'useless passion.' We try hard to disguise this from ourselves by living in the present moment, or allowing ourselves to be carried away by emotions, or simply by telling ourselves lies about the meaning of the universe. Sartre would undoubtedly dismiss Steiner's whole philosophy as a tissue of falsehood and self-deception, 'mauvais-foi'.

But Sartre never seemed to have noticed one interesting fact about human consciousness. In order to perceive something, I have to retreat *inside* myself. An obvious example would be listening to music: many people close their eyes and retreat into some 'mind space' behind the eyes in order to enjoy it. In the same way, if I am deeply enjoying a book, I am no longer sitting in an armchair in front of the fire: I have floated off *somewhere else*.

Now it may seem that this only applies to 'artistic' experience. Surely it is no longer true when I am catching a bus, or eating a sandwich, or waiting for the traffic light to turn green? But a moment's thought reveals this is not so. I enjoy my sandwich most when I am relaxed—'inside myself'. That is why a typist chooses to eat her lunch on a quiet park bench and not in the middle of Piccadilly Circus. When you are tense and irritable, your consciousness has come up to the surface, so to speak, and you see the world as a bewildering mess. If you try to read a newspaper article in this state, you do not 'take it in'; you may have to re-read the same paragraph several times. If you go to an art gallery in this state, you do not really see the pictures. You stare *at* them, but somehow you fail to 'take them in'. And that phrase 'take them in' reveals what we do when we really 'see' something. We take it *inside* ourselves, like a tiger seizing its prey and dragging it deep into its lair.

The explanation for this is quite simple. Our brains contain a giant library of memories—everything that has happened to us during the course of our lives, and even (if Jung is correct) remote racial memories bequeathed to us by our ancestors. If all these memories were set out on shelves, as in a real library, the building would have to be as big as the earth.

Scientists did not become aware of the vast extent of this brain-library until after 1933, when a neurosurgeon named Wilder Penfield made an interesting discovery. He was performing a brain operation on a patient who was wide awake (since the brain has no nerves, it does not feel pain). He happened to touch the temporal cortex—the seat of memory—with a probe that carried a weak electric current. As long as the probe was in contact, the patient experienced a memory of childhood—a memory so precise and detailed that it was like re-living it. Penfield had accidentally caused some of the 'memory tapes' to play back. Each contact of the probe brought back *one single* memory in minute detail.

Now consider a man's experience of his wife. When she comes into the room, he feels he 'knows' her fairly well. Yet if some friend were to ask him to recount in detail the story of their courtship, he would begin to remember all kinds of things he had half-forgotten. And if his wife walked into the room again, he would see her with 'different eyes'. For by reviving these memories he has, in effect, added a dimension of reality to her. We are all familiar with this experience of talking about someone who is not present, and feeling that we have somehow come to know them better.

What Sartre calls 'nausea' is merely *surface perception*. And it tells very little about the world around us. In order to really perceive the world, I must retreat 'inside myself'. In fact, if I can sink into one of those states of inner peace and relaxed meditation that sometimes happen when 'the pressure is off', I may feel that I am really seeing things for the first time. Everything seems to become more rich and complex and interesting. The difference between *this* perception and my everyday perception is like the difference between a Dutch interior by Van Eyck and a Walt Disney cartoon of Donald Duck. I can only achieve this richer, deeper perception by sinking inside myself.

Now clearly, all animals have this capacity to retreat 'inside themselves' to some extent. But it seems a reasonable assumption that in the case, say, of cows or dogs there is not much to retreat into. And there are many human beings who are not much better off—Sartre says of the café proprietor in *Nausea*, 'When his café empties his head empties too'; and of his own father: 'When he looked inside himself he found a desert.' We know that this is not strictly true; no one contains a desert, for we all have an immense library in our heads. But the books are usually inaccessible to us.

The fact remains that human beings differ from all other animals because the world inside them is so much better furnished that that of dogs and cats. Gazing out of the window of a train, I may reflect about my childhood, or about my recent holidays, or a thousand other things, including Sartre and Rudolf Steiner. Of course, much of this thought is mere free association, like drifting in a boat along a slow stream, staring up at the leaves. But the boat also has an engine, and when necessary, I can think to some purpose. I can use my mind to solve problems that would be quite insoluble to an animal.

This is a fairly recent development in man's evolution. Our ancestors who built the first cities around 6000 BC were deeply religious—for some odd reason, man has always been a religious animal—but they did very little thinking as such. They solved problems by common sense and rule of thumb. The first evidence that man was using his mind to try to understand the universe is the Great Pyramid, built around 2600 BC, for there is strong reason to believe that it was a gigantic astronomical observatory whose purpose was to help the priests catalogue the stars. Stonehenge, built at about the same time, whatever other functions it performed, also seems to have been designed as an astronomical computer or calculator.

But it is not until about two thousand years later, in the golden age of Greece, that we begin to encounter real thinking in the modern sense of the word. And, like all great revolutions, it occurred virtually overnight. We only have to read the platonic dialogues to see that Socrates and Plato enjoyed thinking as much as a football fan enjoys the cup final. They did it for pleasure. In the *Symposium* one of the guests at a banquet describes how Socrates once stood in the same place for twenty-four hours thinking about a problem. No doubt this is untrue, but it expresses something essential about the Socratic spirit. It implies that Socrates could forget the external world and take a twenty-four hour voyage *inside himself*. A century later, Euclid spent a lifetime committing all the basic theories of geometry to paper, an activity that would have struck one of the early city builders as unbelievably boring. Yet for Euclid, geometry was plainly as important as meat and drink.

This faculty of thought is so new—for in the evolutionary sense, two or three thousand years is a mere blink of an eyelid—that we have not started to grasp its significance. We all spend years at school learning to read and write; but just under the surface, the primitive cave man wonders what on earth is going on. The cave man is naturally *passive*. He feels himself to be a mere product of nature. When he is hungry, he looks for food; when it rains, he looks for shelter. He merely reacts to problems. But the development of thought has started to turn him into a different kind of creature. Thought is not afraid to try and *control* nature. And whenever he solves an important problem, man experiences a curious flash of exultation, a momentary feeling that he is far more powerful than he realized. Ancient man believed in gods; after the coming of thought, man began to realize that he himself contains fragments of godhood.

These glimpses are usually brief, for the complexity of modern life keeps most of us trapped in 'surface perception'. We tend to feel that we are 'creatures of circumstance', victims of fate. Sartre calls this 'contingency', the feeling that we are somehow unnecessary and superfluous. And this is due, to a large extent, to our feeling that we possess very little control over ourselves. When we get hungry, we feel miserable; when we are tired, we get bad-tempered; when we get tense, we bite our nails. And in moods of deep pessimism, we may feel that life is a long-drawn-out battle with inevitable defeat at the end of it.

Yet even in this state, the power of thought can catapult us back into optimism. We can study the process, for example, in Wordsworth's 'Intimations of Immortality' ode. He begins in a thoroughly pessimistic mood, describing how, as a child, the world seemed to be 'apparelled in celestial light', and how this has all changed: 'The things which I have seen I now can see no more.' 'Heaven lies about us in our infancy', but the 'Shades of the prison-house begin to close   Upon the growing boy . . .'. Yet he goes on to admit that while, on this beautiful sunny day, 'to me alone there came a thought of grief', a 'timely utterance' has given that thought relief, 'And I again am strong.' By thinking deeply about his reasons for gloom, he has *thought* himself back into a feeling of strength and inner certainty. Steiner would say that he has entered the world of thought and achieved a deeper sense of reality. Wordsworth himself expresses the same insight when (addressing his friend Coleridge) he writes:

> Thou, whose exterior semblance doth belie
> Thy soul's immensity . . .

All this begins to explain why Steiner says that entry into the 'world of thought' is the first major step on the 'inward journey' that can lead to 'knowledge of higher worlds'. He argues that although modern man feels he knows all about thinking, he has not even begun to grasp the true nature of that revolution that occurred in the time of Plato. He still feels 'contingent'. His view of himself is still basically negative. This is because he fails to recognize that his inner world is a realm in itself, an interior universe in the most literal sense. He spends too much time in 'surface perception', and feels that the mind is merely a kind of mechanism for helping him to stay alive, as a vacuum cleaner helps a housewife to keep the place tidy. He fails to grasp what Sir Edward Dyer meant when he said 'My mind to me a kingdom is.' This power to take voyages inside himself is new and strange. Where inward journeys are concerned, modern man has only just passed his driving test, and is still too nervous to venture much beyond the end of the street. He actually possesses a completely new power, a new dimension of mobility. Steiner saw it as one of his main tasks to bring this recognition into the clear daylight of consciousness. It explains why his followers were so cheerful and optimistic. They felt that he had given them a piece of extraordinary 'good news'; yet it was a piece of intellectual good news, not something that demanded faith or religious assent.

There is yet another reason for evolutionary optimism. In the past ten thousand years or so, man's survival has been mainly due to his capacity for *concentrating on particulars*. He has developed a sort of mental microscope to enable him to deal with the endless problems and complexities of existence. It has now become second nature, and he peers through it all the time. But the problem is that it limits his field of vision; it traps him in narrow horizons of the present. The chief disadvantage of this microscope is that it causes him to exaggerate all his problems—to make mountains out of molehills. This means that his general view of human existence is far gloomier than it need be. He is always getting himself into 'states' of anxiety about problems that he can overcome perfectly easily.

Whenever some anxiety suddenly evaporates—either through his efforts or of its own accord—he experiences a delightful sense of freedom, the feeling that Chesterton calls 'absurd good news'. And this is not simply because the problem itself has vanished; it is because his relief gives him a sudden 'bird's-eye view' of his own existence, and he is overwhelmed by a sense of distant horizons. He realizes that he has been living in a kind of mental slum when he owns a palace. He sees that *all* the problems on which he wastes so much of his mental energy can be routed just as easily. He sees that his powers are far greater than he believed, and that all that has prevented him from realizing this sooner is this 'mental microscope' that traps him in boredom and triviality. In a paradoxical sense he is already free, already happy, and only a misunderstanding prevents him from realizing it.

What can we do about this? The basic answer was discovered by the modern psychologist Abraham Maslow. It was Maslow who decided to study the psychology of healthy people, and discovered that all healthy people seem to have regular 'peak experiences', delightful sensations of bubbling happiness and freedom. As he talked to his students about peak experiences, they began to remember peak experiences they had had in the past, but had forgotten about almost immediately. And as they began talking and thinking about 'peak experiences', the students began to *have* peak experiences all the time. It was merely a question of thinking about them regularly, turning the mind *in that direction*.

One more point. When Wilder Penfield was conducting his experiment on the cerebral cortex—with the patient still conscious—he discovered that, while the patient was experiencing a kind of mental film of his own childhood, he was also fully conscious of the room around him. This meant, in effect, that *two* streams of consciousness were flowing simultaneously, without mingling. This surprised him because he had always taken the view that consciousness is an activity of the nerve cells (neurons), a mere *product* of the brain. But if that was so, the two streams ought to have mingled, like a hot and cold tap flowing into the same bowl. This seemed to suggest that something was keeping them apart. If the brain is a computer, then it has a 'programmer' who stands *above* its activity. It could be said that Penfield has proved the existence of the soul.

Steiner spent his life fighting scientific 'reductionism'— like the view that awareness is a mere brain activity, as burning is the activity of a fire. He taught that man possesses a 'controlling ego', which is the highest of his 'components'. Half a century after Steiner's death, an American physician named Howard Miller was to arrive at the same conclusion on purely medical grounds.* It would be possible to devote a whole chapter to pointing out how many of Steiner's 'occult' insights have since been vindicated—or at least supported— by modern science.

The fundamental tenet of Steiner's teaching is that if we take the trouble to recognize the independent existence of the inner worlds of thought, and keep the mind turned in that direction, we shall soon become increasingly conscious of their reality. We are not, as Sartre believed, stranded in the universe of matter like a whale on a beach. That inner world is our natural home. Moreover, once we can grasp this truth, we can also recognize that we ourselves possess an 'essential ego', a 'true self', a fundamental identity that goes far beyond our usual feeble sense of being 'me'.

*See my *Frankenstein's Castle*, Chapter 7.

Two

Childhood of a Visionary

RUDOLF STEINER was fortunate in the landscapes of his childhood. He spent his early years surrounded by magnificent prospects of mountains and green plains. Born in Kraljevec in Hungary (now part of Yugoslavia) on 27 February 1861, Steiner later felt it was of symbolic significance that he grew up on the frontiers of east and west. His father, a gamekeeper in the service of a count, left his job when he married, to become a telegraphist employed by the Southern Austrian Railway. He was placed in charge of the station at Pottschach when Steiner was two. It was a boring life, being part of the gigantic official machinery of the Austro-Hungarian empire. But for his eldest son, it had the advantage of being as idyllic as Wordsworth's Lake District.

He was fortunate in another way. All small boys are fascinated by what their fathers do; and the electric telegraph operated by Johann Steiner was the latest and most exciting of nineteenth-century inventions. Invented a mere two decades earlier by Samuel Morse (who also devised morse code), it was the first mechanical instrument to eliminate distance, and make it possible for Vienna to speak to Berlin, London to New York. Even the railway had only recently replaced the coach as a means of travel. So although Steiner grew up in a small country town, he was surrounded by the latest modern technology—in twentieth-century terms it was like being born next to a launching site for space probes. He was later convinced that it was the combination of these two influences—the beauties of nature and the latest modern technology—that created his unique temperament, the blend of the scientist and the visionary.

Steiner's family were Catholics, and he was baptized a

Catholic. Although he says very little about the religion of his childhood in the Autobiography, it is a reasonable guess that it played a vital part in his inner life, and helps to explain why the figure of Christ plays such a central role in his later philosophy.

When Steiner was eight, the family moved again, to Neudörfl, near the border with Lower Austria. This had the considerable advantage of being an hour's walk away from the town of Wiener-Neustadt, in Austria, only twenty-eight miles south of Vienna, where Steiner would later acquire his education. The scenery was less impressive than at Pottschach—the Alps were now on the horizon—but there was compensation in the beautiful woods that surrounded the village. The family was poor, and in summer, Steiner used to go for long walks and return laden with strawberries, raspberries, and blackberries, which formed an important addition to the dinner menu. He even walked to a mineral spring half an hour away with a large clay jar, and returned with a gallon of the sparkling liquid to wash down the noonday meal.

It sounds an idyllic existence; but in reading about it, we have to take into account the sheer dullness of living in the middle of nowhere; life was so quiet for the villagers that they all assembled at the station whenever a train drew up. What a brilliant young mind needed was mental stimulation. And this came into Steiner's life through a volume on geometry, lent to him by the assistant teacher at his school. Bertrand Russell, in his own autobiography, describes how his earliest mental awakening came through reading Euclid, and it is important to grasp that by temperament Steiner was closer to Russell than to Madame Blavatsky. He says:

> That one can work out forms which are seen purely inwardly, independent of the outer senses, gave me a feeling of deep contentment. I found consolation for the loneliness caused by the many unanswered questions. To be able to grasp something purely spiritual brought me an inner joy. I know that through geometry I first experienced happiness.

When he speaks of 'many unanswered questions', Steiner is not referring to great universal problems—like where space ends—but to quite down-to-earth questions that consumed him with curiosity. For example, there was a textile factory close to their house, and its raw material arrived by rail. Steiner was able to see the material when it arrived, and again when it left, but he was never allowed into the factory to see *how* it was transformed from one stage to the other. This was the kind of thing that fascinated him. There was always a strong practical streak in Steiner. If he had been born in America, he might well have become another Edison rather than a 'spiritual teacher'.

It is also interesting to note the way he speaks of geometry as 'something purely spiritual'. He means that it belongs to a *world of the mind*, which is independent of the world of the body. But surely it is a misuse of language to call this 'spiritual'? Here a passage in Arthur Koestler's autobiography may help us to grasp the central point. Koestler admits that he suffers from 'Chronic Indignation' as some people have chronic indigestion. He describes how one day he was sitting on a park bench reading an account of Arab atrocities against Jews in Palestine, and how he experienced the familiar rush of adrenalin into the blood, and the desire to get up and do something violent. At this point, he opened another book about Einstein, and read a sentence that said that the General Theory of Relativity 'led the imagination across the peaks of glaciers never explored before by any human being'. He suddenly saw Einstein's famous formula— $E=MC^2$ —'hovering in a kind of rarified haze over the glaciers, and this image carried a sensation of infinite tranquillity and peace. The martyred pioneers of the Holy Land shrank to insignificance.'

This is clearly what Steiner experienced as he became absorbed in geometry.

I said to myself: the objects and events seen by means of the senses exist in space. This space is outside man; but within him exists a kind of soul-space, which is the setting for spiritual beings and events. It was impossible for me to regard thoughts as mere pictures we form of things. To me they were revelations of a spiritual world seen on the stage of the soul. To me, geometry was knowledge which man himself apparently produces, but its significance is completely independent of him. Of course, as a child I could not express this clearly to myself, but I felt that knowledge of the spiritual world must actually exist within the soul as an objective reality, just like geometry.

Here we have the essence of Steiner's thought. He is saying: If we can develop this capacity to turn to this peaceful, tranquil world of mental objects, we can gradually develop the ability to see more and more distant horizons in this inner world. When I settle down to read a book, I have moved into the mental world, but only into its backyard; my mental horizon remains limited. If the book fascinates me and moves me deeply, I leave this backyard, or ante-chamber, and move deeper and deeper into the mind space inside me. As I do this, I have a strange sensation which could be compared to gliding. It is as if the mind had managed to rise above the turbulent air of daily trivialities, into a peaceful, cloudless realm where it can glide silently, gently rising and sinking with air currents. No one who has ever experienced this sensation can forget it. It seems to promise a completely different kind of life, no longer tied to the 'thousand natural shocks that flesh is heir to'. There is a breathtaking sensation of freedom, and a sense that this is a foretaste of what human existence might become.

What becomes very clear from Steiner's autobiography is that he knew this instinctively. Living in this peaceful environment, watching the seasons change the trees from brown to green, he was able to retreat into the regions of the mind in a way that would be difficult for a modern city dweller. His teacher introduced him to music—he played piano and violin—and taught him to draw. From the village priest he learned about the politics of the Austro-Hungarian empire, and the passionate desire of Hungarians to be allowed to speak their own language and develop their own culture. The same priest gave him a basic knowledge of astronomy, teaching him about eclipses of the sun and moon. Steiner was also profoundly moved by church rituals. Yet his father was a freethinker, so he was confronted by this stimulating contradiction between the world of belief and the world of scepticism. When his father and the assistant station master of a nearby village sat under the linden trees in the evening, they argued incessantly about politics; the young Steiner listened with fascination, observing with amusement that whenever one said Yes, the other said No. Like a tree, his mind was putting down deep roots, seeking instinctively for the nourishment it needed to grow. Science, politics, religion, music—all were absorbed. And when the doctor from Wiener-Neustadt told him about Goethe, Schiller, and Lessing, it was a revelation of yet another new world. By the age of ten, life had become a series of discoveries. Few children can have had the opportunity to develop as gently and naturally as Steiner, absorbing nourishment like a tree.

At the age of eleven, it was time to go to secondary school. Faced with a choice of 'gymnasium', with its classical education, or the 'realschule', with its emphasis on science and technical training, his parents decided on the technical school; they hoped that in due course he would become a railway engineer. This meant daily journeys to Wiener-Neustadt—by train in the morning, and back to Neudörfl on foot in the evening, when there were no suitable trains. 'Shades of the prison house began to close.' The noisy modern city bewildered him, and for the first year at school he did badly. Then, as he began to adjust to the new pace of life, the old voracious appetite for knowledge reawakened. He had a sense that the world was full of a million things he wanted to know, so he read without any specific sense of direction. But at least he had an extraordinary persistency. His headmaster had written a book about physics, in which he tried to explain the attraction and repulsion between planets—and all other physical bodies—in terms of a universe packed with billions of atoms, all constantly banging into one another. From Steiner's account, it sounds as if his headmaster simply failed to grasp the Newtonian theory of gravitation; at all events, young Steiner found it all very stimulating, although he was baffled by the mathematics. When he heard the name of Immanuel Kant, Steiner saved up and bought a copy of *The Critique of Pure Reason* and, totally unprepared by any philosophical training, spent his days trying to master its abstruse arguments. Because he found history classes so boring, he separated the *Critique* into sections, hid them inside his history book, and read them in history lessons. He made up by reading his history direct from the textbooks, and received a mark of 'excellent'.

Fortunately, Kant's philosophy did him no harm. Other German men of genius have been shattered by it; the poet Kleist and the philosopher Fichte were both convinced that Kant's teaching proves that we can never know anything for certain, and had to wrestle with despair. Steiner, with peasant common sense, treated it purely as a stimulating intellectual exercise, and revelled in it. In the same way, he gulped down a nine-volume *History of the World*, and received top marks in the history class.

Steiner was a natural 'autodidact'. He says that his school lessons passed in a kind of dream, but as soon as he began to read what *he* wanted to read, his mind woke up, and he experienced a sense of 'full consciousness'.

By the time he was fifteen, he was so obviously brilliant that he was given the job of tutoring fellow students—not only from lower classes, but from his own. So Steiner was introduced to his life's work of teaching from an early age. He amused himself by playing a game of intellectual hide-and-seek with one of his teachers, Josef Mayer, who taught literature. Steiner somehow discovered that Mayer was an enthusiastic admirer of the philosophy of Johann Friedrich Herbart, an educationalist and psychologist whose views would cause him to be classified today as a 'positivist' (i.e. a kind of materialist). (Herbart has much in common with the twentieth-century thinker John Dewey.) All Steiner's instincts were anti-materialistic. So in his essays, he began expressing views that were opposed to Herbart, without ever mentioning him by name. One essay concluded: 'Such a person is psychologically free.' Mayer looked ironically at his fifteen-year-old pupil and said: 'There is no such thing as psychological freedom.' 'Yes, there is,' replied Steiner, 'There *is* psychological freedom, but there is no "transcendental freedom" in ordinary consciousness.' Mayer said sternly: 'I think you have been reading philosophy. You had better stop—it only confuses your thoughts.' Relations between them, Steiner admits, continued to be strained.

When Steiner was eighteen, he began to attend the Institute of Technology in Vienna. The railway company seems to have been extremely obliging, and agreed to transfer his father to a station—Inzersdorf— sufficiently close to Vienna for Steiner to make the daily journey.

By this time, Steiner had confronted the question that was to be the starting point of his philosophy. The science he loved so much told him that man was an animal, and that animals are machines. This idea revolted him; all his instincts rebelled against it. It contradicted all those strange moods of delight that he had so often experienced among woods and mountains, and which told him that man has the potentiality of becoming a god. One of his closest schoolfriends in Wiener-Neustadt infuriated him by professing to believe that man is a wholly material being, and that all his thoughts can be explained in terms of brain chemistry. One day, Steiner accompanied his friend to the railway station in Vienna, and as the train was about to pull out, tried to express all his detestation of materialism in one passionate outburst. 'You maintain that to say "I think" is merely a result of brain and nerve-processes. You believe that only these processes are real. You think the same thing applies when you say "I see", "I walk", and so on. But please note that you never say "my brain thinks", "my brain sees", "my brain walks". If you really believe in your own theory, you should change the way you express yourself. The fact is that you are lying when you say "I". But you cannot help but follow a healthy instinct that contradicts your own theory. Your actual experience is quite different from the ideas you dream up in your theory. Your very consciousness proves that your theory is a lie.' At that moment, the train pulled out. As Steiner walked back, he experienced twinges of conscience at trying to refute materialism in this crude manner. But what mattered was not just to give philosophically convincing proofs, but to express his total conviction that the human 'I' is a concrete reality. *That* conviction was the foundation upon which he built his immense structure of ideas.

It is hard for us nowadays to grasp just how tormented Steiner felt by scientific materialism—as did so many other great intellects at that time. Yet unless we try to grasp it, we cannot even begin to understand how Steiner came to create the vast system he called 'occult science'. In past centuries, what was taught in schools and universities was the most advanced knowledge of the time, and students could absorb it without any qualms or doubts. In Steiner's time, schools and universities were teaching ideas that seemed to millions of people outrageously untrue. They were teaching—as the latest word in modern thinking—that man is a machine, that religion is a superstition, and that evolution is a purely mechanical process based on survival of the fittest. This made respectable churchmen see red, but their honest indignation only seemed to make things worse. They always seemed to come off worse in arguments with scientists—as when T. H. Huxley wiped the floor with Bishop Wilberforce in the famous Oxford debate on evolution in 1860. (When Wilberforce asked whether Huxley was descended from an ape through his grandfather or grandmother, and Huxley replied that he would not be ashamed to be descended from an ape, but he *would* be ashamed to be connected with a man who used his great gifts to obscure the truth, even hostile members of the audience burst into applause.) So for men like Steiner, who detested materialism yet felt no sympathy with orthodox religion, it was of vital importance to try to find some *scientific* way of refuting the materialists. This is why dozens of pages in the early part of Steiner's autobiography are taken up with descriptions of the philosophers he devoured. He was seeking some argument that would disprove materialism once and for all.

For Steiner, one of the most important of these intellectual allies was the philosopher Fichte. A century earlier, Fichte had been plunged into despair by the philosophy of Kant, which seemed to prove that our senses are liars, and that we can never know 'things as they are'. If that is true, then man is little better than a worm. Then Fichte made an important mental leap. He noticed that, when we sit thinking, we often feel confused and uncertain. But the moment a man is launched into vigorous action, his doubts vanish like mists in the morning sun. According to Fichte, mere thinking is bound to tell us lies, because it puts us into a *passive* state of mind. So when the thinking self says 'I', it is not the true 'I' speaking, only half an 'I'. Let the thinker get up out of his armchair and try to find ways of *living* his thought; only then will his thinking be powerful and accurate.

Fichte's thinking had the bracing effect of a cold shower on the perplexed young student. When some materialist told him 'The ego is an illusion', he could retort: '*Your* ego seems to be an illusion because you won't get out of your armchair. Get rid of your lukewarm scepticism and you'll soon see that the "I" is a reality.'

Even more important was the influence of Professor Franz Brentano, who taught at the University of Vienna, and whose public lectures Steiner was allowed to attend. Brentano not only became a major influence on Steiner's thought, but— through the influence of his follower Edmund Husserl—one of the most important influences on twentieth-century philosophy.

Brentano was concerned at the way materialism had come to dominate psychology. The English philosopher Hobbes had declared that the mind does not exist, for it is a contradiction to talk about an 'immaterial substance'. The Scottish philosopher Hume said that when he looked inside himself, he did not discover some 'essential David Hume', but merely a lot of sensations and ideas, drifting around like leaves in the wind. James Mill asserted that the mind is a machine and that its laws are mechanical. His son John Stuart Mill shrank from this extreme view, but suggested that our thoughts are a matter of 'chemistry'. By the time of Brentano, this view had become known as 'psychologism'. So, for example, according to psychologism, our ideas of good and evil are due to a kind of mental chemistry, just as our ideas of hot and cold are due to a kind of physical chemistry. If this view is correct, then it is inaccurate to talk about a 'mental act'; all 'acts' are really physical.

Like Fichte, Brentano had one simple and powerful insight. He declared: There *is* a basic difference between a mental and physical act. If I slip on the snow and fall flat on my back, that is an *unintentional* physical act. *But there is no such thing as an unintentional mental act.* When I think, I have to think *about* something; I have to focus my mind on it. You could compare all mental acts (thinking, willing, loving, trying to remember something) to a searchlight beam stabbing into the darkness. There is an element of will, of 'intentionality', in all mental activity. So it is quite inaccurate to compare mental activity to chemistry, or to a kind of drifting, like leaves on a stream. It flows purposefully or not at all.

This is exactly what the young Steiner wanted to hear. His whole life so far had been a struggle for freedom, a fight to escape his poverty-stricken working-class existence. Books and ideas had been the beacons along his road. To tell him that man possessed no free will was an outrage to his common sense. Now Brentano was saying the opposite: mental activity is, by its very nature, purposeful. And anybody who has grasped this can also see that our most rewarding mental activity is that which is *most* purposeful. Conversely, the least rewarding is the least purposeful—the kind of listless, bored activity we indulge in when we don't know what to do with ourselves. According to the materialists, there was no real difference between highly rewarding mental activity and bored mental activity. Now Steiner could see that this was obvious nonsense. And such a realization was enough to galvanize him into working with a new determination and optimism.

It must have been a strange, rather breathtaking sensation to feel that he, Rudolf Steiner, knew better than hundreds of distinguished scientists and philosophers. But such a sensation has been experienced by every original thinker when he sets out to express his own vision of truth. 'I must create my own system or be enslaved by another man's,' said William Blake; and by the age of eighteen, Steiner felt he had laid the foundations of his own system.

It was at this point that he met a man who was to exercise a decisive influence on his future: Karl Julius Schröer, professor of the history of German literature at the Technical Highschool. Steiner found his lectures on Goethe and Schiller a revelation. He had learned about Goethe many years before from his doctor friend; but Schröer's enthusiasm brought it all to life. He made Steiner understand the enormous impact that Goethe's arrival made on the literary scene of the eighteenth century—the same kind of impact made by Wordsworth and Lord Byron in the century of Alexander Pope and Dr Johnson. Steiner read *Faust*—in Schröer's edition—for the first time and found it magnificent. Flattered to have such an attentive student, Schöer was soon inviting Steiner to his home, and talking to him about the second part of *Faust*, which he was at present engaged in editing.

Goethe was the single greatest influence in Steiner's intellectual life. Reading *Faust* convinced him once and for all that he could dismiss the materialist philosophers. What must have delighted him even more was that Goethe had shared his own enthusiasm for science, and had created his own non-materialistic philosophy of science. For Goethe, nature was 'God's living garment', and could not be understood except by recognizing that it is constantly in a process of creation. There is a famous story of how Goethe and Schiller met at a meeting of the Natural Science Society. As they left the building together, Schiller remarked that he wished scientists would not make everything so fragmentary and disconnected, because it made it hard to follow. Goethe, who until then had felt no sympathy for Schiller, was struck by this remark, and launched into a description of his own vision of science. 'There is another way of apprehending nature, active and living, struggling from the whole into parts . . .'. But when he went on to explain that he believed that all plants had developed from one original plant, Schiller shook his head. 'That's not an empirical experience. It's just an *idea*.'

Now, as he learned about Goethe's scientific ideas from Schröer, and began to read some of his writings on science for himself, Steiner at last began to develop his own spiritual philosophy.

Before we go any further, it is necessary to take into account another vital thread in Steiner's development. So far, we have considered only his intellectual development and his struggle to disprove materialism; in this respect, his development could be compared with that of many of his contemporaries, from Carlyle and Nietzsche to Bernard Shaw and H. G. Wells. But there was one important respect in which Steiner differed from these distinguished contemporaries. From the beginning, he had been the possessor of a strong psychic faculty. As a small boy, he had been sitting in the station waiting room when the door had opened, and a strange woman came in. Steiner observed that she resembled other members of his family. The woman stood in the middle of the room and said to the small boy: 'Try and help me as much as you can—now as well as in later life.' Then she walked into the stove and vanished. Steiner decided not to tell his parents; he was afraid of being scolded for superstition. But he noticed that his father was sad the next day. Later, he discovered the reason: a female relative had committed suicide not far away. Her death had occurred at the time Steiner saw the woman in the waiting room.

Describing this later in life, Steiner added:

From that time onward a soul-life began to develop in the boy which made him entirely conscious of worlds from which not only external trees or mountains speak to the human soul, but also the Beings who live behind them. From that time onward the boy lived together with the spirits of nature that can be observed in such a region. He lived with the Creative Beings that are behind objects ... and he submitted to their influence in the same way that he submitted to the influence of the spiritual world.

Readers who can accept Steiner's struggle against scientific materialism may find such comments wholly unacceptable. There can be no doubt whatever that most of us feel a healthy reluctance to devote much attention to such matters as ghosts, life after death, the 'supernatural'. The kind of people who take an interest in these things are often gullible or over-imaginative. Yet anyone who decides to study the 'paranormal' in a spirit of scientific scepticism soon realizes that it cannot be dismissed as superstition or wishful thinking. The body of evidence for ghosts, poltergeists, 'second sight', precognition, psychokinesis, telepathy, and 'out-of-the-body-experiences' is simply overwhelming. We have already seen how J. Rhodes Buchanan came to investigate a bishop's claim that he could distinguish brass in the dark by the taste it made in his mouth, and ended by discovering that many of his students could describe the history of an object by simply holding it in their hands. Sensible, ordinary people are always encountering such anomalies, and discovering that they cannot be explained away as delusions.

I have suggested elsewhere* that our remote ancestors probably took these 'psychic faculties' for granted (and, as we shall see later, Steiner also believed this). We have deliberately 'narrowed' our senses to cope with the highly complex experiences of civilized existence. Our ancestors needed a 'sixth sense' to warn them when a wild animal was lying in wait; the modern city dweller would find such a faculty superfluous. The curious case of Peter Hurkos seems to support this view. Hurkos was a Dutch house painter who fell off a high ladder and smashed his skull. When he woke up in hospital, he found that he could read people's minds, and 'sense' the history of an object by holding it in his hand. There was one minor problem: he was totally unable to concentrate on the ordinary affairs of everyday life, with the result that he found it impossible to hold down a job. It was not until someone suggested that he should use his psychic powers on the stage that he solved the problem of how to make a living. It seems conceivable that our remote ancestors were as 'psychic' as Hurkos—and as unable to focus the mind for more than a few mintutes at a time. In teaching ourselves to concentrate, we have voluntarily abandoned that wider sensitivity to the universe that is still possessed by many primitive tribes. 'Psychics' are people who, through some accident of birth or heredity, still possess these primitive abilities.

Yet where Steiner is concerned, this theory raises an immediate problem. Steiner was not in the least unable to concentrate on the affairs of everyday life. His ability to read Kant in his early teens argues a remarkable faculty of concentration. He was an excellent student who gained high marks in science, mathematics, and history. How can all this be reconciled with the 'atavistic' theory of psychic abilities?

Here Steiner himself suggests the answer: that his psychic abilities were the outcome of a profoundly *meditative* temperament. His autobiography makes it clear that he combined his enthusiasm for science with a poetic temperament akin to that of Wordsworth. (In fact, we may recall that Shelley was also a science enthusiast.) Like Wordsworth, he had the

*In *The Occult*, Chapter 1.

ability to enter into profound states of inner peace. He saw no contradiction between these states and his love of science and philosophy: on the contrary, it seemed obvious to him that when we become absorbed in science or philosophy, we retreat into that 'interior castle'.

It is important to understand why modern man has so much difficulty in experiencing the 'reality' of nature as Wordsworth experienced it. In order to cope with his highly complex life, he has developed the *mechanical* part of his being. We might call this mechanical part 'the robot'. When I learn something difficult—like driving a car or speaking a foreign language—I have to learn it consciously, with painful effort; then my 'robot' takes it over, and does it far quicker and more efficiently than 'I' can do it. The trouble with the robot is that he not only 'takes over' the things I want him to do, like driving my car and typing this page; he also takes over many things I would prefer to do myself, like listening to music or going for a country walk. When I am in a hurry I may even eat 'automatically', without really enjoying it. The robot tends to *rob* us of experience.

In *The Doors of Perception*, Aldous Huxley described his experience with the psychedelic drug mescalin. He was staggered as 'reality' suddenly became overwhelmingly *real*. Everything he looked at seemed to exist with an almost painful reality, as if it was throbbing with its own fullness of being. Even the folds in a piece of cloth struck him as infinitely fascinating and beautiful. The mescalin had put the robot out of action, and allowed the mind to see reality 'naked'.

But Huxley made another important point. Mescalin also made him aware of the vastness of his own inner world. He wrote:

> Like the earth of a hundred years ago, our mind still has its darkest Africas, its unmapped Borneos and Amazonian basins. In relation to the fauna of these regions we are not yet zoologists, we are mere naturalists and collectors of specimens . . .
> Like the giraffe and the duck-billed platypus, the creatures inhabiting these remoter regions of the mind are exceedingly improbable. Nevertheless, they exist . . .
> If I have made use of geographical and zoological metaphors, it is not wantonly, out of a mere addiction to picturesque

language. It is because such metaphors express very forcibly the essential otherness of the mind's far continents, and the complete autonomy and self-sufficiency of their inhabitants. A man consists of what I may call the Old World of personal consciousness and, beyond a dividing sea, a series of New Worlds—the not too distant Virginias and Carolinas of the personal subconscious and the vegetative soul; the Far West of the collective unconscious, with its flora of symbols, its tribes of aboriginal archetypes; and, across another, vaster ocean, at the antipodes of everyday consciousness, the world of Visionary Experience . . .

Some people never consciously discover their antipodes. Others make an occasional landing. Yet others (but they are few) find it easy to come and go as they please . . .

Steiner, it seems clear, was one of these rare types of human being who can travel without difficulty in this inner universe.

Huxley goes on to say that there are two methods of visiting this strange continent: drugs (like mescalin) and hypnosis. Steiner's method is certainly related to hypnosis. When a patient is hypnotized, he is persuaded to sink into a state of deep calm, and to forget his links with the physical world. For modern man, this is an exceedingly rare state, for the outer world clamours for so much of his attention that he finally abandons the habit of trying to leave it behind. He could be compared to a parent who has become accustomed to being awakened a dozen times a night by a teething baby, and acquires the habit of sleeping so lightly that the least sound can draw him back to consciousness.

But to visit our inner worlds—even to the extent of becoming deeply absorbed in a book, or listening to music— we have to get rid of this habit of over-alertness. We need to acquire the habit of deep relaxation, of forgetting all our anxieties (most of which, after all, are quite unnecessary). Steiner seems to have been born with this habit, as Wordsworth was, and the idyllic background of his childhood allowed it to become deeply ingrained.

It is exceedingly difficult to follow Steiner into the 'super-sensible worlds' that he describes in his work—although the attempt must later be made. But we can at least understand what he means when he writes: 'To me, the spiritual world was an *immediate reality*. The spiritual individuality of each person was revealed to me in complete clarity.' For most of us have developed some degree of being able to grasp a person's essence, and to recognize intuitively the level of maturity they have achieved. But it is altogether more difficult to understand what Steiner means when he goes on to say: 'When someone died I followed him further on his journey into the spiritual world. One time after the death of a former classmate, I wrote about this side of my inner experiences to one of my teachers at the *Realschule*. He replied in an unusually kind letter, but with not a single word did he refer to what I had written about the dead school-mate.' This is hardly surprising. The schoolmaster must have suspected that it was either imagination or an attempt to impress. Steiner goes on: 'And it was always the same in regard to my experience of the spiritual world. No one was interested to hear about it. At most . . . people would start to talk about spiritualism. Then it was I who did not wish to listen. To approach the spirit in this way was repellent to me.'

And then, in 1879, Steiner made the acquaintance of a man to whom he could speak openly about his spiritual insights, and who was able to reply with insights of his own. Suddenly, the eighteen-year-old visionary no longer felt that he was a solitary misfit in a world of blinkered materialists. A new phase in his life was about to begin.

Three

The Goethe Scholar

TRAVELLING daily from Inzersdorf to Vienna by train, Steiner made the acquaintance of a middle-aged factory worker named Felix Koguzki, who spent his spare time gathering herbs which he sold in Vienna. Koguzki was uneducated but obviously intelligent, and he often expressed his deep religious convictions in thoroughly obscure language. Steiner found him interesting, and deliberately cultivated his acquaintance. Steiner said of him: 'He gave the impression of being simply the mouthpiece for a spiritual content seeking utterance from hidden worlds ... gradually it seemed to me as if I were in the company of a soul from bygone ages who, untouched by civilization, science and modern views, brought me an instinctive knowledge of the past.'

Steiner adds the interesting comment that nothing could be 'learned' from Koguzki in the usual sense, but that 'because he had a firm footing in the spiritual world' it was possible to obtain through him important glimpses of that world. He often visited Koguzki at his peasant home in the village of Trumau, and felt completely comfortable in its atmosphere of simple piety.

The real significance of his meeting with Koguzki is that, for the first time, Steiner could speak openly about his own experiences of spiritual insight without fear of ridicule or the danger of being regarded as a faintly embarrassing crank.

In his autobiography, Steiner does not mention Koguzki's name—it was later discovered through the research of one of his disciples. Unfortunately, this is not true of another acquaintance of the period whose influence on Steiner was crucial. Steiner's friend and follower Edouard Schuré later spoke of this mystery man as 'the master', and said that he was 'one of those potent personalities who are on earth to fulfil a mission under the mask of some homely occupation'. Schuré deduced from Steiner's descriptions that he was an 'Initiate'. All we know is that this man pointed out to Steiner certain passages in Fichte which helped Steiner to see his way clear to refuting the scientific materialism of his contemporaries. Fichte made him feel that the human 'I' is a concrete reality, not an illusion produced by the physical body, and that therefore man has genuine free will, which can be used to penetrate the spiritual reality behind appearances.

In spite of his obsession with the inner worlds of thought—which he identified with spiritual reality—Steiner was no introvert. He seems to have thrown himself into the student life of Vienna with a passion that seems unusual in such a serious-minded youth. He joined the German Reading Room of the Technical Highschool, and was later elected its librarian, then its chairman. As librarian he wrote begging letters to authors asking for copies of their works; through the library and the university he made the acquaintance of many writers and thinkers. In the Autobiography he is inclined to speak about such encounters with a certain poker-faced gravity, as if they were milestones on his pilgrimage to truth. But it does not take much imagination to place oneself in the shoes of this eighteen-year-old stationmaster's son, with no money and no prospects, and to recognize that what really preoccupied him was the question of getting a 'start in life'. What could he hope to become? His father wanted him to be an engineer, but he never seriously entertained that idea for a moment. What then? A schoolmaster—perhaps eventually a university lecturer? That was a possibility. But in spite of his intellectual discipline, Steiner lacked the academic temperament; there was too much of the poet in him. Like all talented young men with no money, he faced the world without any clear idea of what he wanted to do with his life. So he seized every opportunity to meet writers, artists, philosophers, or any professor who happened to have written a book. The instinct for self-expression is as powerful as the instinct for self-preservation.

So Steiner cast out his nets in many directions. He became a regular visitor at the home of Karl Schröer, the man who introduced him to Geothe's ideas. (Steiner said that when he sat alone with Schröer, he always felt there was another present—Goethe.) He made the acquaintance of the brilliant physicist Edmund Reitlinger, who was dying of tuberculosis. He discovered Wagner's music, and had endless discussions with Wagnerians and anti-Wagnerians. He even attended debates in the Austrian Chamber of Deputies and the Upper House, and took a lively interest in the issue that was undermining the unity of the Austro-Hungarian empire: the demand by minority nationalities—like the Czechs and Hungarians—for greater recognition, and the bitter opposition to these nationalist movements by German-speaking Austrians. (Steiner was on the side of the Germans.) He spent much of his spare time in Vienna's famous coffee houses, particularly the Griensteidl Kaffee on the Michaelerplatz (known as the Megalomania Café), where eventually he became the intimate of various poets and composers.

It was Schröer who introduced Steiner to the work of a young poetess, three years Steiner's junior, called Maria Eugenie delle Grazie, who had achieved a degree of fame with her first volume of poems at the age of seventeen. Steiner wrote an article about her in a small newspaper, as a result of which he made her acquaintance and became a member of the literary circle that surrounded her. She lived in the house of a Cistercian priest, Laurenz Müllner, so Steiner found himself once again exposed to the doctrines of Catholism. It is interesting to note that Maria delle Grazie took a thoroughly pessimistic view of the universe; Steiner wrote: 'To her, the ideals that arise in the human heart are powerless against the cruel, senseless and merciless effect of nature, a nature that mercilessly cries out to man's idealism: "Thou art but an illusion, a creature of my own fantasy, which ever and again I hurl back into nothingness."' Yet although such a view was entirely antipathetic to Steiner, he continued to admire the poetess.' I was never inclined to withold my admiration and interest from what I considered great, even when I absolutely opposed it.' And in due course, he came to adopt a version of her view that there is a primal satanic force in the universe.

The Müllner-delle Grazie circle detested Goethe and admired Dostoevsky, so Steiner was subjected to an interesting clash of ideals. Schröer, who had accompanied Steiner on his first visit to the Müllner household, never went there again when he realized how much they were opposed to Goethe. But Steiner enjoyed these conflicts: 'Delle Grazie's house was dedicated to pessimism; it was a place of anti-Goetheanism. When I spoke about Goethe, they listened; but Laurenz Müllner thought that what I attributed to Goethe had fundamentally very little to do with the actual Minister of the Grand Duke Karl August.' And the arguments with the Müllner circle enabled Steiner to formulate his own basic insight. In an article about Maria delle Grazie, he wrote:

> Our ideals are no longer so shallow that they can be satisfied by the all-too-often superficial and empty external reality. Yet I cannot believe that no possibility exists to rise above the deep pessimism this insight can bring. And I find the means to rise above it when I look into man's inner world; that is, when I approach the actual reality of our world of ideas. It is a sphere enclosed and complete in itself . . . Are not our ideals . . . realities in their own right, independent of the favours or disfavours of external nature . . . ?

He goes on to express an idea that makes it sound as if he was reconciled to his own poverty and lack of recognition: 'Where would our divine freedom be if external nature protected us like helpless children, led by the hand? No, external nature must deny us everything so that the happiness we achieve is wholly our own independent creation.' This stoical and ascetic attitude explains why, when he came to encounter the ideas of Karl Marx and Friedrich Engels, he was revolted by the notion that a Utopian society is an end in itself.

Fortunately for Steiner, fate—aided by Karl Schröer—had offered him a means of subsistence. Schröer recommended him as a tutor to the family of Ladislaus and Pauline Specht, and Steiner entered their home in July 1884, when he was twenty-three. They had four children, the youngest of whom, aged ten, was mentally retarded. Steiner soon formed the conviction that the problem with such children is basically physical: the body, not the soul, is undeveloped. This meant that it was a question of trying to draw out the child's mental faculties by slow and patient effort, the first task being to gain

his love. Physically speaking, the child's problem was hydro-
cephaly—'water on the brain'. Mentally speaking, the problem
was a certain self-mistrust, the result of his dullness and
slowness when compared to his brothers. Steiner saw it
basically as a question of giving the child confidence—what
modern psychology calls 'motivation'. It meant considerable
effort on Steiner's part; for example, spending two hours
preparing an hour-long lesson. But he was spectacularly
successful. Within two years, Otto Specht had caught up with
the primary school curriculum and passed the entrance
examination for the Gymnasium. Moreover, the hydrocephalic
condition was steadily improving, supporting Steiner's
conviction that the health of the body depends on the health
of the mind. Steiner remained the boy's tutor for six years,
until Otto was sufficiently developed not to need him. He
became a doctor, and was killed when serving in the First
World War; his mother, who was deeply attached to him, died
soon afterwards.

The experience in education brought Steiner insights that
were to be of use later in the Waldorf schools. For Steiner,
education meant the development of the personality—the
ego—not the mere acquisition of knowledge. He was to
develop the view that man is a fourfold being, consisting of
the physical body, the etheric body (also known as the 'aura'
or life-field), the astral body (which can leave the physical
body under certain conditions), and finally, the ego, which
orders and co-ordinates the other three. In education, as in
health, these four elements must be brought into harmony.
So, in a child like Otto Specht, the basic problem was the
undeveloped state of the ego, which made it unable to
perform its task as 'conductor' of the orchestra. Steiner's task,
in which he was totally successful, was to nurture the ego
until it grew strong enough to take on its proper role. All this
explains why Steiner was so struck by Fichte's emphasis on
the importance of the ego, and why it assumed the central
role in his own philosophy.

This preoccupation with the importance of the ego also
explains why Steiner was aroused to irritation by the philosophy of Eduard von Hartmann, one of the most exciting and
influential philosophers of the day. Hartmann had become

famous at the age of twenty seven (in 1869) with a book called *The Philosophy of the Unconscious*. Since Freud, the term 'unconscious' has passed into the general vocabulary; but in the mid-nineteenth century it was still a startling and fascinating concept. Hartmann believed that the force behind the world is a deep unconscious will, which appears in animals in the form of instinct. Hartmann was opposed to Darwin's mechanical ideas of evolution—*that* appealed to Steiner—and offered in its place the idea of an unconscious life force. But, like his master Schopenhauer, he goes on to reach deeply pessimistic conclusions about human existence. In creating consciousness, the unconscious life force made a ghastly mistake, for reason and 'daylight consciousness' are profoundly opposed to the great irrational force that drives all living things. Man's intelligence has separated him from his instincts, so he is in a position to recognize the sheer futility and meaninglessness of all this instinctive activity. So life is self-defeating; consciousness and the unconscious cancel one another out . . .

It may seem surprising that Steiner was thrown into such a frenzy of opposition by Hartmann's pessimism, which is not, after all, so different from that of Maria delle Grazie, which Steiner had been able to accept quite calmly. We must remember that Hartmann, with his impressive grasp of biology and physics, seemed to be one of the most exciting and up-to-date thinkers of his age, so his philosophy was taken far more seriously than the poems and dramas of a young girl. And Hartmann's view amounted to the belief that life is a 'tale told by an idiot', and that evolution is not only going nowhere, but is undermining itself. For Steiner, this raised the most fundamental of all questions: what is consciousness *for*? According to Hartmann, its purpose is simply to give living creatures more *perception*; it could be compared to the invention of the electric light. In fact, most of us take such a view for granted. Steiner felt instinctively that consciousness is an *active* force, whose purpose is to focus and concentrate on problems. It is not a light so much as a hand that *grasps*. And the hand that grasps can also build and create. It was Hartmann who helped to make Steiner aware that his own philosophy was fundamentally opposed to the whole 'spirit of the age'. Ten years later, he would give these ideas definitive expression in his first major book, *The Philosophy of Freedom*.

In 1883, Schröer had performed another important service for Steiner; he urged an editor named Joseph Kürschner to allow the twenty-two-year-old Steiner to edit Goethe's scientific writings, and Kürschner agreed. It may seem startling that he offered such a task to an unknown student. But we have to bear in mind that the series in which these writings were published— *German National Literature*—was one of those immense popular compilations of the late nineteenth century, running to 221 volumes; it was a response to the demand of ordinary householders for readily accessible classics. Presenting Goethe's scientific writings was a task that few people would have been eager to undertake; there was a general feeling that they were the absurd aberration of a poet of genius. In effect, Steiner was being tossed a scrap that no one else wanted.

Fortunately, Steiner's own basic ideas were in opposition to this negative view of Goethe. Like Goethe, he felt that nature is 'God's living garment', and was profoundly opposed to the current tendency to treat it as a world of dead matter. Steiner himself had no reservations about science; on the contrary, he regarded himself as a scientist. He could enjoy a textbook of physics or mathematics as much as a poetic drama. But he felt that science needed to be redeemed from its materialism.

Now Goethe had, in fact, been a very remarkable scientist; his experiments were precise and well planned, and the conclusions he drew from them were usually accurate. Long before Darwin, Goethe was an evolutionist. He rejected the widely held view that man is in some way totally distinct from all the lower animals. One of the main arguments for this view was that man has no intermaxillary bone in his upper jaw— the bone which, in animals, contains the incisors. Goethe studied skulls and pointed out that man *does* have such a bone, although it is now scarcely visible. His conclusions, now totally accepted, were ignored by contemporary scientists.

But for Steiner's contemporaries, the intermaxillary bone was not the stumbling block. It was not even Goethe's idea about the *Urpflanze*, the original primeval plant, from which he believed all subsequent plants developed. The real embarrassment was Goethe's immense *Theory of Colour*, published in 1810, and describing the results of twenty years of experiment with light. For the purposes of this three-volume work was nothing less than to disprove Newton's theory of light. When he looked at a white door through a prism, Goethe was surprised to find that, instead of turning into an immense rainbow, it remained white, with rainbow colours only around the edges. Goethe jumped to the conclusion that Newton was mistaken in believing that white light is composed of the seven colours of the rainbow. But in that case what *causes* colour? Goethe replied: the mechanism of the eye. After all, it is the mechanism of the eye that prevents a colour-blind person from seeing certain colours. Goethe also placed great emphasis on the phenomenon of 'complementary colours'. If you stare fixedly at a bright yellow object, then look away at a wall, a blue after-image will appear. Staring at a red object will cause a green after-image. This proves, according to Goethe, that the mechanism of colour is in the eye itself. He produced an elaborate theory in which orange is simply a 'darker' version of yellow, and red a darker version of orange, while indigo is a darker version of blue, and so on. Colour is explained as a function of light and darkness.

In a sense, Goethe was simply the victim of a misunder-standing. Newton believed that light is a stream of particles—tiny hard balls—and Goethe could not imagine why white light—a stream of white billiard balls—should actually consist of a stream of coloured billiard balls; it seemed illogical. It was easier to believe in one-coloured balls, and some mechanism in the eye that colours them.

In fact, the Dutch astronomer Huygens had long ago suggested the true solution to the riddle: that light is not made of particles, but waves. Because of Newton's prestige, no one took him seriously. In 1803, seven years before Goethe published his book on colour, the English physicist Thomas Young performed experiments that showed fairly conclusively that light is made up of waves. Unfortunately, Goethe's independent streak inclined him to believe that all the theories so far were nonsense.

Thirty-two years after Goethe's death, in 1864, James Clerk Maxwell finally put forward the theory that would have provided Goethe with the solution he needed. Maxwell argued that light is simply one of many forms of electro-magnetic vibration. There are many forms of this energy, ranging from radio waves with a wavelength of more than a mile, to gamma radiation with a wavelength of less than a thousand millionth of an inch. Our eye is an instrument for detecting a narrow band of radiation whose wavelengths are between sixteen and thirty-two millionths of an inch—light. It cannot distinguish radiation below that—heat—or above it—ultraviolet.

And how does the eye achieve this miracle of distinguishing between such tiny wavelengths? The answer appears to be: by seeing them as 'colours'. It sees light of thirty-two millionths of an inch as red, and light of sixteen millionths as violet. We could say that the eye has 'invented' colour. And if, for some evolutionary reason, it became necessary for us to perceive wavelengths greater than red or smaller than violet, it would invent new colours that do not at present exist.

So Goethe's instinct *was* correct; the eye does invent colour. But Newton was also correct: white light *does* consist of the seven colours of the rainbow.

Steiner could edit Goethe's scientific works with a perfectly clear conscience because he felt that Goethe's attitude to reality was fundamentally correct. He instinctively rejected the view that the 'truth' behind nature is a world of sound waves and light waves and heat waves: 'It drove all spirit from the external world.' Neither could he accept the view of pessimists like Maria delle Grazie and Eduard von Hartmann that the meanings we see around us are merely reflections of our emotions and desires. For Steiner, it was an urgent necessity of life to find *intellectual* grounds for believing that the world of meaning is a spiritual reality. Goethe provided him with precisely what he was looking for. This is why Goethe became, now and henceforward, the centre of Steiner's intellectual life. He was the one undoubtedly great man of the nineteenth century who was totally untainted by materialism or pessimism. In his introductory essays to Goethe's scientific writings (later collected as *Goethe the Scientist*) Steiner hurled himself with enthusiasm into his task of rehabilitating Goethe's vision of nature. And when he had completed the editorial work, he went on to write his first book, *Theory and Knowledge in the Light of Goethe's Weltanschauung,* published in 1886.

Later in life, Steiner was asked by a disciple why he had kept silent about 'occult matters' until he was forty. Steiner's reply was that he had to make a position for himself in the world first, and to acquire the necessary courage. But the impression made upon the reader of these early writings is that occult matters were still far from his mind; he hoped to overturn nineteenth-century materialism and pessimism with purely intellectual tools. They give the impression that Steiner regarded himself basically as a philosopher, like von Hartmann, and that he hoped to create a kind of optimistic metaphysics. This surely explains his obsessive interest in philosophy during this period of his life, and why he read Fichte and Hartmann—and later Nietzsche—with such passionate interest. It is the view of most of Steiner's followers that he was busy laying the foundations of 'spiritual science' from the time he came to Vienna in 1879, and that he devoted himself to philosophy during his earlier period to lay the foundation for his later teachings. It can only be said that the writings themselves provide no support for this view. They suggest that Steiner saw himself simply as a philosopher whose basic task was to make materialism untenable. In these early years, he seems to have hoped that the solution lay in the immense prestige attached to Goethe's name. Later, he came to realize that even Goethe's fame as Germany's greatest writer lent no authority to his views on science; the scientists could simply declare that Goethe was no scientist. When Steiner finally reached this conclusion, he realized that his approach needed rethinking. But in 1886, that time still lay far ahead.

By the mid-1880s, Steiner's enthusiasm for Goethe had given him the 'start in life' he so badly needed; in Austria and Germany, a man who has edited Goethe has established his intellectual credentials, and can never thereafter be dismissed as a nonentity. He was slowly becoming something of a personality in Vienna. He published a few newspaper articles, including the one on Maria delle Grazie which led to their friendship. Physically speaking, Steiner was unimpressive: a small, thin man with untidy long hair and metal-rimmed spectacles; a friend described him as looking like an undernourished seminarian. Socially speaking, he was comically inept and liable to *faux pas*; one upper-class acquaintance mentioned that he used the intimate *du* where it was inappropriate, and that he 'didn't know a thing'. In the 'Megalomania Café' he had long arguments with a young writer named Hermann Bahr, who claimed to be the founder of a new literary group called 'young Vienna', and who represented in Vienna the symbolist and 'decadent' ideas that Oscar Wilde represented in London or Stéphane Mallarmé in Paris. Steiner's instinct was all against them; but, as yet, he was unable to defend his position intellectually.

His circle of friends continued to widen. He became a regular visitor at the house of a pastor, Alfred Formey, where literary and musical celebrities gathered. There he met the widow of the dramatist Hebbel, who gave recitations (presumably from her husband's works), and an actress named Ilma Wilborn, who was soon inviting Steiner to her own 'At Homes'—rather livelier than those of Pastor Formey. Like Goethe, Steiner was deeply interested in the theatre as a medium for presenting ideas—an interest that later came to fruition in his four mystery dramas.

Steiner's circle widened further when, in January 1888, he became the editor of a newspaper, the *German Weekly Review*; it appeared simultaneously in Vienna and Berlin, and had a strongly political flavour. Steiner felt obliged to write and think about politics, although the subject did not come naturally to him. 'I wished to introduce something containing an impulse towards the great spiritual goals of mankind.' Nowadays, an editor who tried to talk about 'great spiritual goals' in a political newspaper would find himself out of a job; but in nineteenth-century Vienna, an idealistic tone was perfectly acceptable. Steiner nevertheless found journalism hard going, and was not sorry when, after six months, the owner of the newspaper quarrelled with its founder, and he lost the job.

His work as a newspaper editor led to an acquaintance with the socialist leader Victor Adler, and many other active socialists. In his usual omnivorous way, he began to study the writings of Marx and Engels. Predictably, he found their materialism distasteful:

> It was impossible for me to find any inner relation to all this. Personally it was painful for me to hear it said that in human history it is the material-economic forces that carry forward man's evolution, while the spiritual is merely an ideal super-structure to this 'truly real' foundation. I knew that the spirit is a reality. To me, what the theorizing socialists maintained meant closing one's eyes to the real facts.

But even at this stage, at the age of twenty-seven, Steiner had still not formulated his ideas clearly enough to be able to express precisely why he rejected dialectical materialism. In spite of his intellectual brilliance, he was still an awkward, earnest young man who could not formulate his deepest convictions in words. Steiner was a slow developer; what he needed was some sheltered environment in which he could develop at his own pace.

In the following year, 1889, he was offered what he needed. On Schröer's recommendation, he was asked to present himself at the Goethe-Schiller Archive at Weimar, to be considered for the task of editing Goethe's scientific manuscripts for the Archive's complete edition. Steiner had little difficulty in convincing the director, Bernard Suphan, that he was the right man for the job. It was arranged that he should start in a year's time.

On the same trip he visited Martin Luther's room in the Wartburg, as well as spending time in Berlin and Munich. There can be no doubt that this first journey into the greater world was of immense importance for Steiner. His natural capacity for floating off into mental worlds meant that every historical site and art gallery was a vital imaginative experience. Most of us find historical sites a fairly superficial experience; the guide assures us that such and such an event took place there, and we take his word for it; but we are more aware of the other tourists and the souvenir shops and the ice cream vans. All his life, Steiner had the ability to enter into the spirit of a place, to conjure up the scenes that had taken place in the past. So in front of Goethe's statue in Weimar he felt that a 'life-giving air was being wafted over everything', while his visit to the Wartburg impressed him so much that he felt it was one of the most memorable days of his life. In these surroundings, Steiner could sense the birth of a spiritual revolution; it is inconceivable that he failed to reflect upon his own role as the spiritual successor of Luther and Goethe.

He went to Berlin specially to meet Eduard von Hartmann— further evidence of his obsession with the ideas of the great 'philosopher of the unconscious'. The meeting was a disappointment. Hartmann was an impressive, bearded man, who, because of a knee ailment, spent most of his life sitting on a couch with his legs outstretched; but he talked with zest and confidence. Clearly, he regarded Steiner merely as a young admirer. 'He did not really inwardly *listen* to what I said.' And Steiner, for his part, seems to have over-reacted. He took exception to Hartmann's idealist view that all we can know of reality comes from the mental pictures it makes on our senses. Steiner replied that he felt we ought to ask whether our mental pictures *are* unreal, only to be told that the very term 'mental pictures' proves it. 'I felt inwardly chilled. "Word definition" as a serious point of departure for a view of life!' This is hardly fair; Hartmann's comment was perfectly reasonable. Steiner's account of the interview suggests that there was no genuine exchange of ideas because he had not yet learned how to formulate his own basic intuitions.

Back in Munich for the winter, Steiner became increasingly interested in a phenomenon that had become the latest intellectual fashion: Theosophy, the system of 'esoteric wisdom' propagated by Madame Blavatsky and her followers. The Theosophical Society had been founded in New York in 1875; ten years later, following an investigation by the Society for Psychical Research, Madame Blavatsky was denounced as a fraud. But her followers remained convinced that she had been 'framed' by her enemies. And in Vienna, the chief of her followers was a wealthy dilletante named Friedrich Eckstein, who had met Madame Blavatsky in London in 1884, the year before the denunciation. He had returned to Vienna with the newly published *Esoteric Buddhism* by A. P. Sinnett, the book that was to convert the Irish poet W. B. Yeats to Theosophy. Steiner almost certainly met Eckstein, who was his own age, in the 'Megalomania Café' in 1888. This was the year that

Eckstein and his fellow Theosophists took a castle, the Schloss Bellevue, for their summer colony, filling it with all kinds of aesthetes, spiritual aspirants, and students of ritual magic. In this circle it was more or less *de rigeur* to be a Wagnerian, and in this respect Steiner qualified; he was always a lover of music. But Steiner was not equally impressed by *Esoteric Buddhism*; he read it in its German translation and professed to find it repellent.

Chief among the Vienna Theosophists were the feminist Marie Lang and her husband Dr Edmund Lang. That winter of 1889, Steiner began to visit their home, and learned more of the doctrines of Theosophy. There was a great deal in it that appealed to him: for example, its belief that the human soul evolves through many incarnations, and that 'salvation' is actually a process of self-realization. Sinnett declares that Theosophy sees no need to keep science and religion in separate compartments; physics and spirituality are not only reconcilable, but interdependent; this was Steiner's own profound conviction. Theosophy teaches that the spirit evolves through a chain of worlds or planets—again a doctrine to be found in Steiner's later work. Steiner's account of the after-death process, with the soul's progress through 'Kamaloca' (or purgatory), is again very close to that to be found in *Esoteric Buddhism*. And Steiner, like the Theosophists, accepted the doctrine of reincarnation; he explains in the Autobiography that it became increasingly obvious to him as he talked to various people and sensed intuitively that some of their qualities could not be explained either in terms of heredity or experience since birth. (For example, he felt that there were qualities in the poet Ferther von Steinwand that could only have developed at a remote epoch when Greek paganism coexisted with Christianity.)

All this explains why Steiner later became so deeply involved with the Theosophical Society. What is far more difficult to determine is how far his own ideas were derived from Theosophy, and how far he developed them for himself. He says of *Esoteric Buddhism*: 'I was glad that I had not read it until after I had attained spiritual perceptions of my own.' Inevitably, Steiner's hostile critics regard such statements as attempts to hide the extent to which his own ideas are derived from Madame Blavatsky and Sinnett. And it is certainly difficult to point to concrete evidence that proves the contrary. Steiner's anti-materialism first found expression through his admiration of Goethe. But it also seems clear that Theosophy exerted a far greater influence than he was willing to admit.

It is necessary to make an imaginative effort to understand why Theosophy exercised such a wide appeal. A century after the death of Madame Blavatsky, it seems to be generally agreed that she was a mixture of charlatan and literary genius, and that works like *Isis Unveiled* and *The Secret Doctrine* are Christmas puddings into which she tossed every possible ingredient from Buddhism to the Atlantis myths. But in the late nineteenth century, there was a deep and powerful craving for some great religious revival. There was a general feeling that materialism and agnosticism had gone too far, and that it was time for a backswing of the pendulum. Old-fashioned Victorian Christianity was not likely to take on a new lease of life; but the natural religious impulses of man were bound to rise up in some new form, and bring mankind back to a perception of spiritual realities. Once again, religion would triumph over materialism, just as Christianity had triumphed over the paganism of the Romans. There was an intense feeling of *expectancy*—not so much of some new messiah as of some new messianic doctrine. This explains what we shall otherwise find very difficult to understand: why Steiner's doctrines later spread with such speed across Europe. But before Steiner came along, the major candidate in the 'new religion' stakes was Theosophy. Madame Blavatsky's *Isis Unveiled* was too long and complex to exercise any wide influence. But Sinnett's *Esoteric Buddhism*, with its claims about hidden wisdom derived from Mahatmas in Tibet, was a literary sensation; it went through edition after edition. In 1885, the world had not grown cynical, as it was to do a century later. Yeats read the book, handed it to his friend Charles Johnston, and Johnston was so excited that he rushed off to London immediately to get permission to set up a Dublin branch of the Theosophical Society. In Vienna, Eckstein was the bearer of the torch. It is important to note that men like Sinnett, Johnston, and Eckstein were not dubious cranks; they were regarded as respectable members of society with sound intellectual credit. If they could accept hidden masters in Tibet, so could thousands of other respectable middle-class people.

Now Steiner was, beyond all doubt, a man who possessed his own spiritual vision; in that basic sense, he was indebted to nobody. From the beginning, he experienced a powerful sense of 'the unseen world'. But he was also a natural 'intellectual', a lover of philosophy and science and mathematics. A young man with strong intuitions that run counter to the prevailing temper of his age, looks around for allies, for men he can set up as models. Steiner's natural allies should have been the great mystics of the past, men like Eckhart, Boehme, Swedenborg. But he had no patience with mystics because they were not scientific enough; they insisted that their visions were 'ineffable'. By the time he had reached his mid-twenties, Steiner had found only one 'ally'—Goethe.

So the advent of Theosophy was bound to make him thoughtful. It was carrying the doctrines of spiritual evolution to a far wider audience than Steiner could ever reach with his books on Goethe. Eckstein records that Steiner asked him to explain the doctrines of Theosophy in 1888. We know that Steiner eagerly read *Esoteric Buddhism* soon after this; he apparently found its doctrine of 'secret masters' a little too 'materialistic'. But in the following year, he became a regular visitor at the home of Marie Lang, and decided that 'within herself she had a store of mystical knowledge which life's hard trials had caused to become conscious in a spontaneous way.' So although Steiner continued to have reservations about Theosophy, particularly in the form in which it was presented by a rather dishonest 'occultist' named Franz Hartmann, he was persuaded by Marie Lang that it deserved taking seriously.

All this made Steiner decide that it was time he tried to set out his own 'philosophy of spiritual activity'. He discussed it with a new friend, the feminist writer Rosa Mayreder (who is remembered nowadays mainly as the librettist of Hugo Wolf's opera *Der Corregidor*). From what Steiner says about her in the Autobiography, it seems clear that there was no real intellectual sympathy between them. 'My attempt to reach conscious experience of the spiritual on the basis of acknowledged science could not possibly appeal to her'; and, again, 'Nor did Rosa Mayreder find my relation to art in the least satisfactory. In her opinion I misunderstood the essence of art...'. That Steiner could nevertheless find her a sympathetic companion, to whom he could pour out the ideas later embodied in *The Philosophy of Freedom*, seems to indicate that he craved an audience. 'She partly relieved the inner-loneliness I felt.' At twenty-eight, Steiner lacked self-assurance. The thin, bespectacled young man, who still looked like a 'half-nourished seminarian', was grateful for the sympathy and attention of an older woman, even if she thought most of his views *were* nonsense.

In that last year in Vienna, Steiner felt that an epoch of his life was drawing to a close. The future in Weimar looked bright and promising. At this point, Steiner had no suspicion that his seven-year exile in the city of Goethe would be little more than a period of marking time.

Four

The Long Apprenticeship

STEINER was an exceptionally slow developer. It is probably
safe to say that if he had died before his fortieth birthday, he
would now be totally forgotten. Unlike Yeats, whose 'chosen
comrades thought at school   He would be a famous man',
Steiner seems to have failed totally to convince any of his
early friends that he was a potential genius—or if he did, we
have no record of it. He was a withdrawn, introverted young
man, so inept at expressing his feelings that one of his closest
friends was convinced that he was cold-hearted. The same
friend also considered him a rationalist, because he seemed to
spend so much time wrapped up in his own thoughts. In the
Autobiography, Steiner himself admits that while knowledge
of the spiritual world always struck him as self-evident, he
had considerable difficulty coming to terms with the real
world. He found it 'difficult to relate . . . to the world of the
senses'. A psychiatrist would probably have diagnosed him
as a mild schizophrenic, schizophrenia meaning a lack of
contact with reality.

In a sense, therefore, the young Rudolf Steiner was a
typical figure of the *fin de siè*cle period—a romantic dreamer
who never seemed quite at home in the physical world. Yet in
one important respect, he was far more fortunate than so
many contemporaries in that 'tragic generation'. Most of them
also felt alienated from physical reality; but their 'inner lives'
also failed to satisfy them. They felt like dissatisfied strangers,
'outsiders', shipwrecked in the world of actuality. Steiner had
no such problem. He may have felt awkward and out of place
in the physical world, but he never had the slightest doubt
that his inner world was just as real as external reality. His
genuine enthusiasm for ideas saved him from falling into the

despair that wrecked or destroyed so many of his contemporaries.

In Weimar, that 'Athens of the north', to which he moved in the autumn of 1890, he needed all his self-sufficiency. There was, admittedly, a great deal of lively social activity—although never as warm and intimate as in Vienna—and Steiner made many friends. But as a 'spiritual home', Weimar was a disappointment. The spirit of Goethe—the feeling that nature is God's living garment—was totally absent from the Archive. Men like Bernard Suphan, Hermann Grimm, Julius Wahle, Eduard von der Hellen, Reinhold Koehler, were pleasant enough, but Steiner felt that the underlying spirit of the place was pedantic. In a short time he was referring to Weimar as 'the home of the classical mummies', and telling Eckstein (whom he called Eck): 'You can have no idea how alone I feel here, and how little understood.' Soon after arriving in Weimar, Steiner gave a lecture entitled 'Imagination as a Creator of Culture', in which he argued that 'what man creates in real imagination is in fact a product of the spiritual world'. From what Steiner says of his colleagues in Weimar, we may infer that it was received with bemused incomprehension.

Yet in another sense, the spiritual isolation was a benefit. In Vienna there were too many friends, too many cafés, too many distractions. In Weimar, there was little to do but develop his ideas. Even with friends like Julius Wahle and Eduard von der Hellen, Steiner could not speak about his spiritual experiences. He seized the opportunity to work on his *Philosophy of Freedom*—a book whose title suggests it was intended as a counterblast to Hartmann's *Philosophy of the Unconscious*—and to write a thesis for his doctoral degree.

Since he was now a staff member of the Goethe Archive, it was important that he should acquire some academic qualifications. The problem was that, since he had not attended the Gymnasium in Vienna, he was not eligible for a degree. But in Germany, regulations were, oddly enough, less rigid. During his final days in Vienna, Steiner had read with enthusiasm a vast work called *The Seven Books of Platonism* by a certain Heinrich von Stein, of the University of Rostock, a Baltic sea port. It excited him because it 'presented Plato as the great bearer of a philosophy that awaited fulfilment through the Christ impulse'. Perhaps because he sensed that von Stein was a sufficiently original thinker to recognize another when he saw one, Steiner decided to send him his thesis: 'A Theory of Cognition, with special reference to Fichte's scientific teaching'. In May 1891 he travelled to Rostock to defend his thesis—in those days a part of the formal machinery for acquiring a degree. Von Stein proved to be old, serene, and tolerant. He told Steiner: 'It is obvious that you have not been under the guidance of a professor.' But he liked the thesis and accepted it.

Typically, when the thesis was published the following year, Steiner dedicated it to Hartmann. Steiner disagreed fundamentally with Hartmann, and—as we have seen—their encounter in Berlin had failed to bring about any meeting of minds. But Steiner, always modest, still hoped to achieve some degree of mutual understanding with his eminent contemporary.

The same modesty—amounting almost to lack of self-confidence—seems to explain his relationship to another influential thinker, the biologist Ernst Haeckel. Like T. H. Huxley, Haeckel had taken up the cudgels on behalf of Darwin at a time when Darwin was being denounced as an infidel. In fact, Darwin was neither an atheist nor a materialist; Haeckel was both. Like Hartmann, he possessed the ability to write highly readable prose, and his *Riddle of the Universe* became a bestseller.

The two became acquainted by a misunderstanding. Haeckel called his philosophy monism, meaning that the physical world is the only reality, and that 'spirit' is a kind of by-product of matter. Steiner also claimed to be a monist, but he took a diametrically opposite view: that spirit is the only reality, and that matter is a by-product of spirit. In February 1893, both Steiner and Haeckel happened to give lectures on 'monism' to a scientific society, and Haeckel sent Steiner a copy of his talk. Steiner reciprocated by sending his own lecture to Haeckel. In the following year, Steiner was invited to the celebrations for Haeckel's sixtieth birthday; he was introduced to the sage, and found him 'a fascinating personality'. Steiner concluded that Haeckel's 'gentle gaze could absorb sense impressions only', and that he was incapable of real thinking. He reached the interesting conclusion that in some previous existence Haeckel had been a fanatic 'related to Church politics' (i.e. an Inquisitor), and that this tendency combined with his natural gentleness to make him a fanatical opponent of religious dogmatism.

Steiner thereafter defended Haeckel in print on a number of occasions—a circumstance that caused bafflement to many of his later followers. It was obviously impossible that Steiner could have had the slightest intellectual sympathy for a man who declared 'There is no God, no immortality and no freedom of the human soul.' And Steiner's rather patronizing remarks about Haeckel in his Autobiography make his sympathy more puzzling than ever. Steiner's attitude can only be understood by recognizing what Edouard Schuré later called his 'empathetic and feminine sensibility'. He was a modest man with a gift for friendship, so he found himself leaning over backwards to defend views that had nothing in common with his own.

Why underline this point? Because the Autobiography, written in his final years, gives the impression of a man whose philosophical and spiritual views were already fully formed when he came to Vienna at the age of eighteen, and who thereafter marched undeviatingly towards his intellectual goal, without glancing to right or left. But the picture that emerges from comments by his contemporaries, and from his own early work, is quite different. They suggest a shy, modest, socially inept but highly ambitious young man, determined to obtain a hearing from his contemporaries, but not sure how to go about it. Hartmann and Haeckel both provided models—not because Steiner agreed with what they had to say, but because both were immensely successful. And Steiner also, presumably, wished to be successful, an ambition that no one would suspect from the austere pages of the Autobiography.

Another case in point is that of Anna Eunicke, the widow Steiner married in 1899, and from whom he separated when he met Marie von Sivers. During his first two years in Weimar, Steiner had not been particularly happy with his lodgings. Then he was introduced to the recently widowed

Anna Eunicke who, according to one biographer,* asked him
to supervise the education of her five children. Steiner moved
into her home (he was given his own part of the house) and
he and the widow became close friends. When he moved to
Berlin in 1899, the Eunicke family soon followed, and Steiner
again became their lodger; then, shortly thereafter, he married
Anna Eunicke, who was eight years his senior.

Clearly, Frau Eunicke played an important part in Steiner's
life, and one might expect him to devote a certain amount of
space to her in the Autobiography—at least as much, say, as
he devotes to Maria delle Grazie, Rosa Mayreder, Gabriele
Reuter, and other female friends. But he is strangely reticent.
He tells us that, through the family of Dr Heinrich Fränkel, a
liberal politician, he met 'yet another family', whose father
had recently died. There follows a lengthy anecdote about
Steiner's own curious relation with the dead man, of which
we shall speak in a moment. After several more pages, Steiner
mentions that the name of the dead man was Eunicke. Only
then does he devote a few brief lines to the family in whose
house he went to live, mentioning that he and the widow
became close friends, but omitting any mention of his role as
educational adviser of the children. Finally, at the end of a
chapter about his struggles in Berlin, he mentions casually that
'shortly afterward my friendship with Frau Eunicke was
consolidated in civil marriage'. Then he adopts a distinctly
defensive tone:

> Let this suffice in regard to a private relationship. In this
> account of my life, it is not my intention to relate private
> matters, except those that are in some way connected with my
> spiritual path. And my life with the Eunicke family afforded
> me the opportunity of a quiet basis for a life that was both
> inwardly and outwardly extremely eventful. For the rest, a
> person's private life does not belong to the public. It is of no
> concern to the public.

All this may be conceded; yet once again the reader is left
with the vaguely uncomfortable impression that Steiner the
human being has been edited out of existence to make room

*Stewart C. Easton, *Rudolf Steiner, Herald of a New Epoch*, p.54

for the more impressive portrait of Steiner the spiritual prophet, standing with folded arms and looking into the distance.

But the story of the deceased Herr Eunicke takes us once again to the very heart of the Steiner enigma. In the Autobiography, Steiner claims that he was in contact with Herr Eunicke after his death. Yet the contact was not of the kind we might expect from a man who had once seen the ghost of a relative in a station waiting room. Steiner explains that when he moved into the Eunicke household he became interested in the deceased father through the books in his library. Herr Eunicke had apparently been something of a recluse, and Steiner became increasingly intrigued by his personality. Something almost identical had occurred eight years previously in Vienna, when Steiner had been introduced to the family of a fellow student. The father spent most of his time locked up in his study, and Steiner never even caught a glimpse of him. Yet when the father died, Steiner felt he knew him so intimately that he was asked by the family to deliver the funeral oration.

This sounds straightforward enough: Steiner became deeply interested in this man who had turned his back on the world, asked many questions about him, and gradually came to feel that he knew him intimately. But, as the Eunicke story makes clear, there was a great deal more than that to it. 'What I [now] have to say will be regarded by most people as sheer fantasy. For it will concern the way I was privileged to come into close contact with these two human souls in that sphere where they found themselves after they had gone through the gate of death.' And he goes on to remind the reader that 'I have always approached spiritual knowledge in the same state of clear consciousness as is necessary for the pursuit of such exact branches of knowledge as mathematics or analytical mechanics . . .'.

But when Steiner says he will describe 'the way' he came into contact with the two dead men, he is speaking loosely. He merely informs us: 'The powers of spiritual sight which I then possessed enabled me to enter into a close relationship with these two souls after their earthly death.' We are told no more about the precise means by which he was able to follow their progress after death. Instead, he tells us that although both men were 'materialists'—as far as their intellectual approach to life was concerned—they did not *act* like materialists (i.e. they were not ruthless or unsympathetic men). The result was that 'the spirit of both men ... shone with wonderful light after death'.

In a lecture of 1918, 'The Dead Are With Us', he is much more forthcoming. In this, he emphasizes the similarity between sleep and death. He goes on:

> Besides waking life and sleeping life there is a third state, even more important for intercourse with the spiritual world ... I mean the state connected with the act of waking and the act of going to sleep, which last only for brief seconds ... If we develop a delicate sensitivity for these moments of waking and going to sleep we shall find that they shed great light on the spiritual world ... At the moment of going to sleep the spiritual world approaches us with power, but we immediately fall asleep, losing consciousness of what has passed through the soul.

In order to understand all this, says Steiner, it is necessary to grasp a basic fact about the spiritual world.

> In the spiritual sense, what is 'past' has not really vanished, but is still there. In physical life men have this conception in regard to space only. If you stand in front of a tree, then go away and look back ... the tree has not disappeared ... In the spiritual world the same is true in regard to *time*. If you experience something at one moment, it has passed away the next as far as physical consciousness is concerned; spiritually conceived, it has not passed away. You can look back at it just as you can look back at the tree. Richard Wagner showed that he possessed knowledge of this with the remarkable words: 'Time here becomes space.'

In this lecture Steiner certainly shows no reticence about the matter of intercourse with the dead. (He adds, in parenthesis: 'The methods of modern spiritualism, of course, must be avoided ...'.)

We encounter the Dead at the moment of going to sleep and

again at the moment of waking . . . As far as physical consciousness is concerned, these are two quite different moments in time; for spiritual consciousness the one is only a little further distant than the other.

He goes on to say that the moment of falling asleep is specially favourable for communication with the dead. If we wish to ask something, we should 'carry it in the soul' until the moment of sleep, then put the question. The moment of waking is the best moment for the dead to communicate with us. The question must be imbued with feeling and with will. Then it will be committed to the 'subconscious', and will be automatically passed on to the dead at the moment of falling asleep.

There is another rather confusing piece of information. When we put a question to the dead, what we say actually comes from the dead person: the answer comes from us. The dead inspire the question, so to speak, and the answer comes from our own soul. This, says Steiner, is the reason why, although we are constantly surrounded by the dead, we cannot communicate with them—we are unfamiliar with this curious back-to-front language (which, admittedly, sounds like something from *Alice in Wonderland*). This also explains why, when the dead communicate with us at the moment of waking, we may be unaware that they *are* communicating; we simply assume that *we* thought it. 'A great deal of what we undertake in life is really inspired by the dead,' says Steiner.

What are we to make of all this? The reaction of someone who comes to it for the first time is bound to be one of deep scepticism; it sounds as if he has made it up for the consumption of a particularly gullible audience. But anyone who has looked into these matters more closely will be aware that Steiner's comments are less bizarre than they sound.

To begin with, Steiner's method of communication with the dead seems to have much in common with that of another eminent 'spiritual scientist', Emanuel Swedenborg, who lived two centuries earlier. Swedenborg (1688–1772) also claimed to be able to establish direct contact with the 'spirit world', and his methods also had nothing in common with those of modern spiritualism. One brief anecdote will suffice. The queen of Sweden asked Swedenborg to give a message to her dead brother. Next time he saw her, Swedenborg told her that her brother sent his greetings, and apologized for not answering her last letter. He would do so now. Swedenborg then delivered a long and detailed message. The queen turned pale and said: 'No one but God knows this secret.'

In his book about Swedenborg, *Presence of Other Worlds*, the American psychologist Wilson van Dusen advances the interesting hypothesis that Swedenborg's 'visions' of the spirit world were obtained in a 'controlled hypnogogic state'—a hypnogogic state being the twilight realm between sleeping and waking, or vice versa. The whole book could be regarded as detailed support for Steiner's assertion that the secret of communication with the dead lies in these hypnogogic states.*

Another 'scientist of the invisible' was the Cambridge don T. C. Lethbridge, who devoted his retirement to the study of dowsing and similar mysteries of the 'paranormal'. † Lethbridge became convinced that a pendulum—a lead bob on a piece of string—will respond accurately to various substances (lead, silver, tin, garlic, oranges, potatoes), swinging over them in a circle when the pendulum is adjusted to the correct 'rate' for any particular substance. (For example, it responded to tin at 28 inches, alcohol at 26, cherries at 12, apples at 18, and so on.) He further discovered that the pendulum also has 'rates' for abstract ideas, like love, hate, anger, death, and so on. Everything he tested responded at some length between one and forty inches. Forty was the 'rate' for death. Yet, oddly enough, if he lengthened the pendulum over forty inches, all the substances began to register again—at a rate of forty *plus* their previous rate (so cherries now reacted at 52, apples at 58, and so on).

For reasons too complex to explain here, Lethbridge came to the curious conclusion that when the pendulum was extended beyond forty inches, it was responding to the world beyond death—the 'next world', so to speak. Lethbridge did not regard this as some other 'place', up in the sky for

*For a more detailed discussion of hypnogogic states, see my *Mysteries*, Part 2, Chapter 5.
† See *Mysteries*, Part 1, Chapters 1-4.

example. He believed that it interpenetrates our present world, but has a much faster rate of 'vibration', so we cannot see it.

Through the use of the pendulum, Lethbridge also came to some curious conclusions about time in this 'next world'. Time exists there, he concluded, but is completely 'static'. Time in the next world is a perpetual 'now'. He speculates that this world is a kind of museum, in which all events are preserved, as in the BBC's sound archives. This sounds very close indeed to Steiner's comments about time in the world after death.

That other great teacher of the twentieth century, Gurdjieff, seems to have made no comment on Steiner and his 'spiritual science'. But a story told by his follower J. G. Bennett makes it clear that Gurdjieff's views on communication with the dead were almost identical with Steiner's. In his autobiography, *Witness*, Bennett tells how deeply he was affected by the death of his mother. One day, Gurdjieff said to Bennett: 'She is in need of help, because she cannot find her way by herself. My own mother is already free, and I can help her. Through her your mother can be helped, but you have to bring them into contact.' He gave Bennett a photograph of his own mother, and said: 'For half an hour every day you practise what I say. First look well at this picture until you can see my mother with your eyes shut. Then place two chairs side by side, and on the right chair picture my mother and on the left your own mother. Stand in front of them and keep your attention fixed upon the wish that they may meet and that your mother may receive help.'

Bennett found the task unexpectedly painful.

After a few weeks the effort of standing for half an hour before two empty chairs became almost intolerable. To my surprise I found myself bathed in sweat . . . as if I had been doing heavy manual labour. One day I burst into tears and sobbed for the entire half hour. Yet nothing at all seemed to be happening. I was invaded with doubts, and a feeling that the whole affair was a cruel joke . . . Then a change began. After I had done the exercises for a month, I began to be aware that there were presences in the room. These presences, which at first were fleeting and nebulous, took the shape of my mother and

Madame Gurdjieff. I felt distinctly that my mother was resisting . . . Then, one day, the contact was unmistakable. A wave of relief and gratitude flowed through me. It seemed at that moment that Gurdjieff was with me . . .*

Steiner's comment that the living are often influenced—at the unconscious level—by the dead can also be found in an early classic of spiritualism, *The Spirits' Book*, by Allan Kardec. Kardec, whose real name was Leon Rivail, was a French polymath of the mid-nineteenth century. In the very early days of 'spiritualism', Kardec heard of a friend whose two daughters could produce automatic writing at will. The daughters were instructed to ask the 'spirits' a number of questions that were written down by Rivail. Many subsequent investigators have found this method highly unsatisfactory, and have ended with large quantities of repetitive drivel. Rivail was lucky. The spirits answered his questions with detailed precision, and the result was a remarkable philosophy of the meaning of human life and the relation of the dead and the living. Rivail's informants told him that the universe is pervaded by incorporeal intelligences. Human beings are simply 'incarnate' spirits. They advance towards perfection through the trials and problems of their lives, and, after death, they are reincarnated in another body, and continue their slow evolution. All this corresponds with great precision to Steiner's teaching. Rivail's informants added that the influence of spirits is far greater than most people suppose; they can enter freely into our minds and influence our thoughts and actions. In extreme cases, this influence amounts to 'possession'. But such cases are rare, and the domination always involves a certain degree of co-operation with the 'possessed' person.

But perhaps the most important and revealing parallel is with an American contemporary of Rudolf Steiner, Thomson Jay Hudson, whose book *The Law of Psychic Phenomena* (1893) is one of the great forgotten masterpieces of the late nineteenth century. Hudson, a newspaper editor and official of the Patent Office, was fascinated by hypnosis, and the extraordinary powers it seems to be able to unleash in otherwise unremarkable individuals. He was also fascinated by such

Witness, p. 254–5.

anomalies as 'calculating prodigies'—children who can calculate enormous sums in their heads in a matter of seconds—and men with 'photographic memories'. These convinced Hudson that the powers of the human mind are far greater than most of us realize.

Hudson came to the conclusion that man possesses two minds: he called these the objective and the subjective mind. The objective mind is the part of us that deals with everyday life; it looks outward, towards the external world. The subjective mind is the part of us that deals with our inner world; it operates largely through feeling and intuition.

Hudson was convinced that hypnosis puts the objective mind—the 'everyday you'—to sleep, and allows the powers of the subjective mind to operate freely. Normally, they are shy and repressed. When they try to operate under the critical gaze of the objective mind, they suffer from a kind of stage fright. But when the objective mind is put to sleep, the subjective mind becomes capable of the most remarkable feats. Hudson watched with amazement as a young man under hypnosis produced the most dazzling philosophical ideas, in the conviction that he was holding a conversation with Socrates.

Hudson believed that all so-called psychic powers— telepathy, clairvoyance, healing, precognition—are the perfectly normal powers of the subjective mind. He decided to experiment with his own healing powers, directing them towards a relative who suffered from such severe arthritis that he was confined to a wheelchair. Hudson decided that the best moment for the use of these powers was on the point of falling asleep at night, or waking up in the morning. The relative experienced an extraordinary recovery, which began from the time Hudson began this healing 'treatment'.

Steiner possessed the same conviction about man's 'hidden powers', and in the Autobiography, quotes with approval a comment by his friend Ludwig Laistner: 'People do not have as much as an inkling of the real significance of the creative power within the human soul. They do not realize that the creativeness of man is an expression of the same cosmic power that creates in nature.'

Hudson is so significant because in the second half of the

twentieth century, his theory of the 'two minds' has been placed upon a scientific basis by experiments in 'split brain' physiology. It had been known for a long time that if the corpus callosum—the bridge of nerves connecting the two halves of the brain—is severed, it can cure epilepsy. What puzzled the surgeons who performed this operation was that it appeared to make no difference to the patient, who went on behaving much as usual. An experimenter named Roger Sperry was among the first to notice that if a split brain patient banged into a table with the left side of his body, he did not notice the impact. For some unknown reason, the left side of the body is controlled by the right side of the brain, and vice versa. Further anomalies began to come to light. One split brain patient tried to hit his wife with his left hand, while the right hand tried to hold it back; another tried to unzip his flies with one hand while the other tried to do them up. It slowly became clear that the ego—the person you call 'you'—lives in the left cerebral hemisphere of the brain, while the person who lives in the other half is, relatively speaking, a stranger. A split-brain patient who was shown a 'naughty' photograph with her right brain (i.e. left visual field) blushed; when asked why she was blushing, she replied truthfully: 'I don't know.' It was that other person—in the right brain—who was blushing.

Why do split-brain patients not realize they have had the operation? Clearly, because in a certain sense, they were split-brain patients *before* the operation. So are we all. The right brain—the 'other you'—deals with intuitions, with 'overall meanings', with patterns; it is the part of us that appreciates music and poetry. The left brain studies the world through a microscope; it is obsessed with the 'here and now'. It deals with language, with logic, with calculation.

There *are* certain moods when the two halves of my brain work so close together that they can actually feel one another's presence. When I am deeply relaxed, when I am in a mood of 'appreciation', I seem to relax *into* the right brain. In these states, I become far more intuitive. My memory works better.

There is some evidence then, for assuming that the right brain is Hudson's 'subjective mind', and that the left brain is the 'objective mind'.

The most important observation to arise from all this is that most civilized human beings spend their lives *trapped* in the left brain, obsessed by the need for efficiency, for 'coping' with the outside world. They can never relax very deeply; they are rather like a man waiting for the telephone to ring, subconsciously remaining in a state of inner-tension.

Artists, poets, mystics, are natural 'right brainers'. So are all children up to the age of seven. (It has been established that in children below that age, the left and right halves of the brain can act interchangeably.) Wordsworth pointed out that as we grow up, 'shades of the prison house' begin to close. We lose that ability to retreat into the Garden of Eden of the right brain; the need to cope with the hard world of adulthood keeps us in a state of tension, listening for the telephone.

All this enables us to understand Steiner's ideas about the 'spiritual world' with far greater precision. These ideas are certainly the greatest stumbling block for the average person. We can understand what Steiner means when he says that there is an inner 'soul space' in all men, and even what he means when he says that this 'soul space' is the setting for spiritual beings and events. What we find quite incomprehensible is how that same soul space is the setting for the ideas of geometry and philosophy and science. What on earth have these to do with 'spiritual beings and events'?

But if we think of 'soul space' as being Hudson's 'inner world', the world of the right brain, we can begin to see what Steiner means. When human beings relax deeply, they can journey into that inner world. A child deeply absorbed in a book is 'in' the soul space. But most of us find it very difficult to venture very far into the inner world; it is as if we were attached to the objective world—and the objective mind— with a long piece of rope. We can relax to some extent; then we reach the end of the rope and have to stop. When we experience some enormous relief, or when someone fascinates us deeply and we become 'absorbed', we cut the rope and walk deeper into that unknown world inside us.

So what Steiner is saying is quite simple. When I become fascinated by a book or by an idea, I retreat into my inner soul space, and this is a *valid* experience of that soul space. But if I can cut the rope, and wander far into that inner land—like

Blake's 'mental traveller'—I shall encounter some very strange landscapes indeed.

Moreover, and this is the central point, the more deeply I wander into that mental land, the more deeply relaxed I become, *and the more deeply intuitive*. That land of the subjective mind is quite unlike the harsh daylight of the objective mind; its contours are gentler, softer; its colours are more subtle, its daylight is closer to our twilight. It is at twilight that our intuitions often operate most powerfully. And in this land of intuition, we may suddenly realize that we 'know' all kinds of things that were simply overlooked or ignored in the harsh glare of daylight consciousness.

Now as soon as we have succeeded in cutting the rope and relaxing deeply into that mental realm, it becomes perfectly obvious that Steiner was right about one thing at least. This *is* a new kind of experience, not just an intensified version of what we experience when we withdraw behind a newspaper or relax in the bath. This deeper relaxation gives us a new feeling of *freedom*, and we experience new kinds of perceptions. We realize that the 'rope' had given us a completely false idea about this inner world, just as we would have a false idea about some land over the border if we had never ventured more than a few hundred yards inside it.

Even highly intelligent and perceptive individuals can make this mistake. It is instructive, for example, to study H. G. Wells's attitude to the problem. In the opening chapter of his *Experiment in Autobiography*, Wells remarks that he is not getting enough freedom and peace of mind to get on with his work. He goes on: 'Entanglement is our common lot. I believe this craving for a release from bothers, from daily demands and urgencies, from responsibilities and tempting distractions, is shared by an increasing number of people.'

He then points out that since life began, most individual creatures have been 'up against it', absorbed with the mere struggle to stay alive. Now, for the first time in history, there is a new type of creature: a human being who wants to live a *mental* life. 'People can ask now what would have been an extraordinary question five hundred years ago. They can say: "Yes, you earn a living, you support a family, you love and hate, but—*what do you do*?"'

Wells compares these 'new men' to the earliest amphibians, struggling out of prehistoric seas to live on the land, seeking to breathe in a new fashion. 'At last it has become for us a case of air or nothing. But the new land has not yet definitely emerged from the waters and we swim distressfully in an element we wish to abandon.' Or, to put it another way, we might say that these amphibians still have flippers instead of legs, so half an hour on land tires them out, and they need to get back to that sustaining element of the sea.

Steiner would reply: You are mistaken. We already have legs. The problem is simply that you have forgotten to *cut the rope*.

In order to understand Steiner, we must try to focus on the very heart of this problem. We must try to grasp what is wrong with us. Man has evolved by becoming more efficient. Being efficient involves a certain *balance* of right and left brain. For example, after many years of practice, I am a fairly efficient writer. I can, for example, read a book from beginning to end in a couple of days, then write a review of it. In order to write the review, I have to allow my right brain to grasp the book *as a whole*—from a 'bird's eye view', so to speak—and then select certain intuitions, certain insights, and translate them into words with my left brain. The two must work in concert. And a certain degree of *tension* is necessary. If I spend two weeks reading the book in a leisurely way, and write the review in the same expansive frame of mind, I shall probably write ten times as much as necessary, and have to prune it. On the other hand, if I am in too much of a hurry, my tension will become self-defeating and I may miss the whole point of the book. I must establish a balance between these two extremes. If I am a busy man, I may carry this same balance into most of my daily activities, from driving my car to eating my dinner. It may, in fact, become my 'normal' state of consciousness. Sitting in my armchair after a meal, I may be quite convinced that I am relaxed, while the old tensions continue, a mere inch or so below the surface of consciousness.

If I face some appalling crisis, which suddenly disappears, then I breathe a deep sigh of relief, and I *really* relax. I 'cut the rope'. And, if I am lucky, I shall recognize that this new relaxation is a vitally important experience. It renews my vitality, strengthens my inner powers. And I shall make it a priority to try to establish these states of deep relaxation by an act of will.

It is, however, far more probable that I shall get a good night's sleep, and simply forget about the experience. The next day, I shall be back in the old state of consciousness, accepting a vaguely uncomfortable state of tension—like a man listening for the telephone—as an acceptable substitute for relaxation.

Steiner was one of those lucky people—Wordsworth was another, and Blake yet another—who are born with the ability to 'relax into the right brain'. He did not achieve this ability, as so many of the Romantic poets did, at the expense of his normal efficiency. In later life, he was capable of a formidable amount of work and concentration. But when it was over, he did not, like the rest of us, settle into an unsatisfactory state of semi-relaxation. He had explored that mental world; he knew it existed. He cut the rope, and crossed deep into that mental land inside himself. And he never ceased to try to explain to his fellow men: You are mistaken to treat the 'world of the mind' as if it were merely a metaphor, or a dim reflection of the physical world. It is *another country*, and we all have passports to cross into it.

There remains one more question to be cleared up. What does Steiner mean when he says that intercourse with the dead involves asking the questions they put into our heads, and receiving their answers from within ourselves? Here again, our knowledge of the process of deep relaxation provides the answer. When I know someone very well, a kind of telepathic contact is established—so, for example, we may both start to say the same thing at the same time. Who puts it into the other's mind? That is impossible to say. And when I am in a deeply relaxed, deeply intuitive state, I *see* the answers to questions, just as a calculating prodigy sees the answer to a mathematical problem. I answer the question myself.

Steiner has also remarked on the importance of the sleeping state. In sleep, he says, we enter the 'spirit world'—although, since we are unconscious, we know nothing about it. If we could carry consciousness into the world of sleep, we would be able to explore the spirit world. Unfortunately, consciousness tends to blank out shortly after we have entered that 'other world'. Perhaps, at some future stage of man's evolution, we shall be able to maintain ego-consciousness while we sleep. Meanwhile, our closest acquaintance with that world occurs on the point of sleeping and waking. Again, what we know of deep relaxation indicates that this makes sense.

When Steiner moved into the home of Anna Eunicke, he was (in Dante's phrase) at precisely 'the middle of the road of life'. He was thirty-two years old, and he had thirty-two more years to live. His entry into the Eunicke household has a symbolic importance, for he later emphasized the importance of his contact with the deceased Herr Eunicke for the writing of *The Philosophy of Freedom*. We could regard *The Philosophy of Freedom*, published in the following year, 1894, as the beginning of a completely new phase in Steiner's life. It is a conscious attempt to lay the cornerstone for all his future work. Steiner's biographer Hemleben says that it 'embodies, purely in the form of thought, essentially everything that was to be the content of the anthroposophy that Steiner developed later.'

Today this book appears less revolutionary than it seemed at the turn of the century because other philosophers— Edmund Husserl, Maurice Merleau-Ponty, Karl Popper, Michael Polanyi—have carried out Steiner's intention far more thoroughly. That intention, quite simply, is to undermine 'reductionism', that temptingly simple theory that tries to explain the mind in terms of physical mechanisms.

Where Steiner was concerned, the problem went back to that day in Vienna when he accompanied his friend to the railway station, and the friend maintained that thought is merely a result of processes in the brain and nervous system. As the train pulled out, Steiner shouted: 'Your very consciousness proves that your theory is a lie.'

But does it? Not according to the reductionists, one of whom, the psychologist J. B. Watson, even went so far as to say that he had never observed such a thing as consciousness. What he meant, of course, was that in his laboratory, studying rats and guinea pigs, he had never observed anything that could not be explained as a *mechanism* of the brain and nervous system. And if someone had replied: 'But what about *your* consciousness—are you telling me that doesn't exist?', he would have replied: 'No, but I am telling you it is a mechanism of the brain and nervous system.'

So the central problem is to *prove* that some psychological process cannot be explained in terms of mechanisms—that it involves free will.

The question is: does it matter? Watson would have said no. But many highly intelligent men of the nineteenth century would have passionately contradicted that view, for they knew that reductionism can cause insanity and death. Fichte described his own deep depression when he read Kant and concluded that 'we can know nothing'. He escaped the dilemma by recognizing that man does not know himself fully until he launches himself into action. (To this, of course, Watson would reply: 'That proves nothing—we all know a car works better when the engine has had time to warm up.') The poet Kleist came close to insanity as a result of reading Kant, and ended by committing suicide. The philosopher William James plunged into a state of profound depression in which he felt permanently frightened and exhausted. He rescued himself by recalling Renouvier's definition of free will—that I can *choose* to go on thinking about something, or I can decide to think about something else. That finally convinced James—he could see no way that the reductionists could get around that particular argument. He recovered from his nervous breakdown and began to work on his definitive *Principles of Psychology*.

All subsequent arguments, by Husserl, Merleau-Ponty, Popper and the rest, depend basically upon this argument about freedom of thought. What they are attempting to show, basically, is that creative thinking cannot be explained in 'mechanical' terms, as if the brain is merely a computer. Creativity involves hovering *above* the subject, like a bird, and seeing many possible choices. Then the bird plunges, like a hawk, and seizes one of these possibilities—when it might just as well seize another. And we are, of course, talking about the difference between 'left-brain thinking' and 'right-brain thinking'. In order to demonstrate that man possesses genuine freedom of choice, we only have to grasp the way in which he thinks creatively, with the right brain using its 'bird's eye view' to perceive a hundred possibilities, and the left deciding which of these it will choose.

Steiner, of course, knew nothing about the left and right hemispheres of the brain, or even about Hudson's objective and subjective minds. He goes, nevertheless, straight to the heart of the problem:

> Materialism can never offer a satisfactory explanation of the world. For every attempt at an explanation must begin with the formation of *thoughts* about the phenomena of the world. Materialism thus begins with the *thought* of matter or material processes. But in doing so it is already confronted by two different sets of facts: the material world and the thoughts about it.

So thought has, in a sense, come out of nowhere—or out of freedom.

The sad truth is, of course, that for the thoroughgoing materialist, this argument would be equally unconvincing. His reply might be somewhat as follows: 'Look at gnats moving on the surface of a pond. Their movements are so complicated that they seem a proof of freedom of choice. Yet if we knew enough about a gnat's brain and about the situation, we would be able to predict every movement, as we can predict a moth's movement towards a candle flame. Someone who could look into the interior of the brain would see thoughts and feelings swarming like gnats; but this does not prove they are 'free'; a scientist with enough information could predict every one of them . . .'.

This sounds like stalemate, until we return to Renouvier's original definition of free will as my ability to sustain a thought or change its direction as I choose. It is impossible to reduce *that* to a will-less mechanism.

The truth is that Steiner's *Philosophy of Freedom* would not convert a single materialist, or give him a moment's uneasiness. But from Steiner's point of view, that was unimportant. All that mattered was that, as a 'scientist', he had established his own logical *foundation*. Now if anyone should accuse him of wishful thinking or irrational optimism, he could point to his book and flatly deny the charge.

To Rosa Mayreder, Steiner wrote: 'I know the exact place

where my book belongs in the current of present day spiritual developments, and can point out the exact spot where it carries Nietzsche's line of thinking further.' Sadly, none of Steiner's contemporaries noticed this. Eduard von Hartmann, to whom Steiner sent one of the first copies, read it carefully, filled it with notes, and still failed to understand a word of it. He sent his copy back to Steiner, evidence that he had no desire to re-read it, with the bewildering statement that it ought to be called *Epistemological Phenomenalism and Ethical Individualism*.

The problem was simple, and it enables us to grasp just why Steiner baffled so many of his contemporaries. Hartmann believed that what we 'see' is a kind of illusion. We might compare this view to the notion that man is trapped inside his own head, watching pictures of the world outside on a television monitor. He can never walk out into the street and see things 'as they really are'. Hartmann assumed that Steiner started from the same basic premise. But this was untrue. For Steiner, man is *already* in the street outside. In his autobiography, Steiner expresses his aim with admirable clarity:

> I tried to show in my book that nothing *unknowable* lies *behind* the sense-world, but that *within* it is the spiritual world. And I tried to show that man's idea-world has its existence within that spiritual world. Therefore, the true reality of the sense-world remains hidden from human consciousness *only* for *as long as* man is merely engaged in sense perception.

This explains why Hartmann failed to grasp Steiner's meaning. He could see that Steiner was admitting that reality usually remains hidden from human consciousness; but he failed to understand the reason. Steiner goes on to say: 'When to the experience of sense-perception is added the experience of ideas, then consciousness experiences the sense-world in its objective reality.' In other words, a dog or cat might fail to grasp the true reality of the sense-world, because they are incapable of handling ideas. But man has the ability to stand back from the chaotic reality of the senses, and to see things in perspective.

Steiner was by no means being muddled or conceited when he compared himself to Nietzsche, and claimed to have gone a step further. For Steiner, human consciousness is not a mere passive mirror, at the mercy of the bewildering confusion of sense-impressions. Man is more like the conductor of an orchestra, *in charge* of consciousness, and of the sense-impressions. Like Nietzsche's Zarathustra, Steiner felt that man can afford to hold his head high; he is stronger than he thinks. Where Steiner goes beyond Nietzsche is in his clear recognition that the source of that strength lies in his 'access to inner worlds'.

It was Steiner's tragedy that the sheer originality of that message was far beyond his contemporaries.

Five

Rebirth

HIS book *The Philosophy of Freedom* marked a turning point in Steiner's life. 'During the first chapter of my life I was destined to experience the riddle of the universe as it faced modern science; in my *Philosophy of Freedom* I formulated the ideas demanded of me by this experience... Now I faced the task of formulating ideas that would present the human Soul's experience of the spiritual world itself.'

And on the threshold of this new epoch in Steiner's life we must ask the fundamental question: *how* did he go about gaining access to the 'spiritual world'?

A vital clue is offered by his friend and disciple Friedrich Rittelmeyer:

> In earlier years, it seemed to me that when he was giving advice to people, he liked to sit where he would not be obliged to look against the light. When he began to use his faculties of spiritual sight one noticed a certain deliberate adjustment of his being, often accompanied by a lowering of the eyes. One remembered then what he says in his books, namely that the physical body of a man must be wiped out before the 'higher members' can be perceived.'*

In other words, Steiner deliberately withdrew 'into' himself, 'wiping out' his perception of the external world. He says elsewhere:

> When, with spiritual perception, I observed the soul-activity of man: thinking, feeling and willing, a picture of a 'spiritual man' became clearly perceptible to me ... I saw these inner manifestations of life as creative forces and they revealed to

*Rudolf Steiner Enters My Life, p. 71.

me 'man as spirit' within the spirit. If I then looked at the physical appearance of man, I saw it supplemented through the structure of spiritual forces, active within the physically perceptible.

Steiner adds another interesting clue: that in these moments of spiritual perception, he experienced a *flood of warmth.* This is important because it is an experience that most of us have shared. Listening to music, reading poetry, kissing a baby, listening to rain pattering on the windows, can all bring that strange, exhilarating flood of happiness and warmth. And in the case of a favourite piece of music or a poem, it is not difficult to see how it happens. The music or poem has certain *associations,* and as we relax and enjoy it, these associations come flooding out. This in turn describes the experience described by Proust: 'I had ceased to feel mediocre, accidental, mortal . . .'.

Even more significant is the experience of the Hindu saint Ramakrishna. As a child, he was crossing a paddy field when a flock of white cranes flew across a black storm cloud: the sight struck him as so beautiful that he collapsed in a faint. Undernourishment may, of course, have had something to do with it, but this does not obscure the central point. Ramakrishna was born with a tendency to 'spirituality'; the beauty of the cranes against the storm cloud brought a flood of 'associations', and a sense of 'access to inner worlds' that produced a sudden and total relaxation—and loss of consciousness. As a young priest, Ramakrishna fell into a state of despair because he had ceased to experience these floods of insight; he seized a sword with the intention of killing himself when 'suddenly the Mother revealed herself to me . . . The buildings . . . the temple and all vanished, leaving no trace; instead there was a limitless, infinite shining ocean of consciousness or spirit.'

From this time on, any mention of the Divine Mother or of Krishna could send Ramakrishna into this total ecstasy which the Hindus call *samadhi.* The name itself was enough to conjure up the flood of associations.

Steiner tells no similar story about how he first learned to gain 'access to inner worlds', and we may infer that there was no single event, but a great number of experiences of this inner-warmth. Music, for example, played a central part. 'Music became all-important for the kind of spiritual experience I wished to establish on a secure foundation within myself.' So did poetry, particularly that of Goethe and Schiller. So at a fairly early stage, by his mid- or late-teens, Steiner had acquired the same basic knack as Ramakrishna: of being able to retreat into himself and cause an instantaneous flood of inner warmth.

The career of the Silesian mystic Jacob Boehme affords another clue. His biographer records that, when Boehme was twenty-five (in 1600), his eyes fell on a pewter dish whose dark surface reflected the sunlight. Like Ramakrishna, he went into ecstasy, and experienced the sensation that he was looking into the heart of nature. He went out into the fields, and felt as though he could see *into* the trees and grass, as if they were made of glass and lit from within. Steiner's own account of 'spiritual vision', while more down-to-earth in tone, reveals that he is speaking about the same thing:

> While in earthly life man develops from birth onward, he confronts the world with his power of cognition. First he gains insight into the physical sphere. However, this is but the outpost of knowledge. This insight does not yet reveal everything the world contains. *The world has an inner living reality* [my italics] but man does not reach this living reality at first. He shuts himself off from it. He forms a picture of the world which lacks inner reality because his own inner reality has not yet faced the world. The world-picture he forms is, in fact, an illusion. As man perceives the world through his senses he sees an illusion. But when, from his own inner being, he adds sense-free thinking to sense perception, the illusion is permeated with reality; it ceases to be illusion. Then the human spirit experiences itself within man and meets the spirit in the world; the latter is no longer hidden from man *behind the physical world; it weaves and moves within it.*

The last phrase—italicized by Steiner—makes it clear that the experience he is describing is identical with Boehme's vision of the 'signature of all things' (by 'signature' Boehme meant the inner reality). Steiner is asserting that once man has learned to create that curious glow of inner warmth and to *retreat into it*, the world ceases to be an 'illusion', and becomes a spiritual reality, permeated with its own vital spirit.

Most of us can grasp what he means. Every nature poet has described the sensation: the feeling that the earth is alive with meaning. We experience it ourselves on a spring morning, when everything seems to glow with a new life. But we are inclined to dismiss this as a 'manner of speaking'. We feel that our own sense of warmth and excitement is *conferring* warmth and excitement on nature. Steiner is denying this view, and stating that what we see in these moods is closer to the reality than what we see in ordinary perception.

What emerges very clearly is that Steiner's attitude is fundamentally romantic, as romantic as Keats, or Shelley, or Hoffmann. This is nowhere more apparent than in his next major work, *Friedrich Nietzsche, Fighter for Freedom*. Steiner had come across Nietzsche's writings in Vienna in 1889, and had become increasingly fascinated by his ideas. This in itself is difficult to understand, since it would be hard to find two thinkers with less in common than Steiner and Nietzsche. Steiner was convinced of the existence of a spiritual world that somehow runs parallel with this one; Nietzsche was convinced that the only world is the one we live in, and that people refuse to face this reality because they are too weak. According to Nietzsche, if people had more strength, more courage, more willpower, they would glory in the existence of 'this world', and recognize that all 'other worlds' are delusions conjured up by weakness and neurosis. This conviction was not the result of intellectual analysis, but of a number of experiences of overpowering ecstasy, moments in which Nietzsche was swept away by a Dionysian flood of strength and optimism; it was after one such moment, on a Swiss mountainside, that Nietzsche conceived the idea of Zarathustra, and wrote on a slip of paper 'Six thousand feet above men and time'. It seems a fair assumption that Nietzsche would have dismissed Steiner as what he liked to call an 'other-worlder'.

Steiner, for his part, admits that he was at first repelled by Nietzsche and by his self-assertiveness: 'I loved his style, I loved his daring, but I did not love the way he spoke of the most significant matters without entering into them.' But then, Nietzsche was a visionary who was convinced that he had seen the truth about human existence. That truth is that man is slowly evolving towards the Superman, and that the sooner he recognizes this and directs all his efforts towards it, the sooner he will forget the religious fairy stories that keep him weak and deluded.

The rather more dubious side of Nietzsche's 'evolutionism' is his glorification of the warrior—particularly when, as an exemplification of the warrior-hero, he chooses an archetypal 'spoilt brat' like Cesare Borgia. Nietzsche's own physical weakness and consequent inability to escape the atmosphere of the study leads him to take a rather unrealistic view of the man of action.

Then how could Steiner bring himself to admire Nietzsche? The answer can be found in the Autobiography:

> I felt him to be a personality who was compelled by disposition and education to live intensely in the cultural and spiritual life around him, but who also felt: 'What has all this to do with me?—so much repels me. There must be a different world, a world where I can live.' This made him a fiery critic of his time, but a critic made ill by his own criticism.

This view seemed to be confirmed when Steiner met Nietzsche. The philosopher's sister, Frau Elizabeth Förster-Nietzsche, came to the Goethe Archive to ask advice about founding a similar Nietzsche archive—her brother had been insane since 1889—and took a liking to Steiner. He was invited to her home, and that of Nietzsche's mother, in Naumburg. On the first visit, he was taken in to see Nietzsche. 'He was lying on a couch. His exceptionally beautiful forehead was that of a thinker and artist. It was early afternoon. His eyes, though dying, still reflected his soul; they took in his physical surroundings, but this no longer reached his mind. One stood there, but Nietzsche was not aware of one's presence. Observing his intelligent features one could believe they belonged to someone who had spent all morning engaged in thought and now wished to rest awhile.'

Steiner now experienced another of his 'spiritual insights':

> The inner shock I experienced led to what I can only describe

as an insight into the genius of Nietzsche whose gaze, though directed towards me, did not meet mine. The very passivity of this gaze, resting upon me for a long time, released my inner comprehension . . . In inner perception I saw Nietzsche's soul as if hovering over his head, infinitely beautiful in its spirit-light, surrendered to the spiritual worlds it had longed for so much but had been unable to find before illness had clouded his mind . . . Previously I had *read* Nietzsche. Now I saw the actual bearer of ideas from the highest spirit realms, ideas that even here shone in their beauty despite having lost their original radiance on the way. A soul who had brought from former lives on earth golden riches of great spirituality but was unable to let it shine fully in the present life. I admired what Nietzsche had written; now I saw his radiant spirit behind what I so greatly admired.

In fact, what Steiner saw in Nietzsche was largely a reflection of himself. *He* felt of his own age: 'What has all this to do with me? There must be a different world, a world where I can live.' Nietzsche had conceived his own philosophy of Dionysian strength in his student days, after taking shelter from a storm in a hut where a shepherd was killing a goat; the crash of the storm mingled with the bleating of the goat and the smell of blood, and brought an overpowering ecstasy which expressed itself in the words: 'Lightning and tempest are different worlds, free powers without morality. Pure will, without the troubles and confusions of intellect—how happy, how free!'

All this is a long way from the romantic, world-rejecting Nietzsche that Steiner 'saw' that day in Naumburg, with his 'golden riches of great spirituality' (a phrase that would have made Nietzsche wince). In spite of which, the book Steiner wrote on Nietzsche—and published in 1895—is remarkably perceptive. It reveals Steiner's extraordinary power of empathy —at times, the style even sounds like Nietzsche. And the reason is that, in spite of their many differences, there *is* a certain basic kinship between Nietzsche and Steiner. To grasp this kinship is of central importance in understanding the essence of Steiner's thought. It can be found in a passage in his earlier book *On the Theory of Knowledge Implicit in Goethe's World Conception.* There* Steiner attacks the view that

*Chapter XI.

the world of thought is dim and unreal compared to the world of sensations:

> The truth is entirely overlooked that mere 'beholding' is the emptiest thing imaginable, and that it receives content only from thinking . . . When one who has a rich mental life sees a thousand things which are nothing to the mentally poor, this shows as clearly as sunlight that the content of reality is only the reflection of the content of our minds, and that we receive from outside merely the empty forms. Of course, we must possess the inner power to recognize ourselves as the creator of this content . . . .

Here we could say that Steiner has already grasped the essence of Nietzsche's Zarathustra, four years before he came across Nietzsche's writings. This is even more clear in the penultimate chapter of the book, which deals with Optimism and Pessimism. Here Steiner states: 'Man is the central point of the world order . . . Things really *are* only as they are illuminated by him. This point of view declares that man possesses within himself the central essence of his own existence. It makes him a self-sufficient being . . .'. And he goes on to dismiss optimism, which says the world is basically good, and pessimism, which says it is bad. 'The external world is, in itself, neither good nor bad; it only becomes one or the other through man.'

This is why, in spite of basic differences of approach, Steiner could write so sympathetically about Nietzsche. Like Nietzsche, his fundamental message is that man is far *stronger* than he realizes. The mind itself transforms reality, as the sun transforms the world when it rises in the morning. As Blake said: 'The fool sees not the same tree that the wise man sees.'

But we should also bear in mind that the book in which Steiner made these assertions is about the 'theory of knowledge implicit in Goethe's world conception'. He is not speaking in his own person, as Rudolf Steiner, but as a kind of mouthpiece for Goethe. In the book on Nietzsche, he is speaking as mouthpiece for Nietzsche. At this point, in his mid-thirties, he has still not acquired the courage to express his convictions in his own voice. And in fact, his next major work—published two years after the Nietzsche book—was yet another study of

Goethe, *Goethe's Weltanschauung*.

Oddly enough, this final—and most definitive—work on Goethe was written as a result of Steiner's friendship with a circle of Nietzsche enthusiasts, the von Cromptons, one of Weimar's most prominent families. Steiner's book on Nietzsche made him a welcome visitor. The von Crompton circle was outspokenly critical of Weimar, which they found 'human, all too human'. They wanted to know how German culture could develop when Weimar, the home of Goethe, made so little effort to fulfil its mission.

Goethe's Weltanschauung differs from Steiner's earlier books in its sense of intellectual passion; at last, he is daring to raise his voice, and speak with a warmth that must have made his fellow Goethe scholars raise their eyebrows. The reason, he explains in the Autobiography, is that he was strongly under the influence of the von Crompton circle, particularly their discussions about the nature of human personality. But he had already grasped this important matter in the earlier book on Goethe. There, after declaring that the 'content of reality is only the reflection of the content of our own minds', he went on: 'Of course, we must possess the inner power to recognize ourselves as the creator of this content; otherwise we shall forever see only the reflection, and never our own mind which is reflected. Indeed, one who perceives himself in an ordinary mirror must know himself as a personality in order to recognize himself as the reflected image.' (He might have added that very few animals recognize themselves in mirrors.) All of which is to say that until I dare to recognize myself fully as an individual personality, I shall never understand that *unconscious creativity* which transforms the world around me. Now Steiner was allowing that realization to overcome his natural modesty—and his caution as a scholar—so that the Goethe book rings with a new depth of personal conviction.

There is, of course, irony in the fact that he still has to take refuge behind Goethe. But Steiner himself was intelligent enough to grasp that irony. He was slowly becoming aware that, whether he liked it or not, he would soon have to stand before his audience as Rudolf Steiner, and dare to use the word 'I'.

It was at this period, when he was writing the final Goethe

book, that 'a profound transformation began to take place in my inner life'. The chrysalis was slowly turning into a butterfly. What happened was that Steiner ceased to feel the need to shrink away from the real world and take refuge in his mental world. It was a kind of rebirth.

> I became able to observe physical things and events more accurately and completely than before. This was the case in regard to scientific investigation, and also to external life in general . . . There awakened within me a new awareness of sense-perceptible things. Details became important. I felt that the sense world has something to reveal which *it alone* can reveal. I felt one ought to learn to know the physical world purely through *itself* without adding any of one's own thoughts.

These remarks sound oddly commonplace for such a climactic change. We have to bear in mind Steiner's admission that he always had great difficulty coming to terms with the real world, as if his sense organs were somehow too weak to make proper contact. For modern readers, that sentence 'I felt that the sense world has something to reveal which *it alone* can reveal' may bring to mind Aldous Huxley's description of his experience under mescalin: that sense that the world has suddenly become fifty times as *real*, and that the sheer 'is-ness' of things is *speaking* to us. Our senses filter the real world, and 'turn it down' like the volume control on a radio; mescalin removes the filter and turn up the volume. This seems to be what Steiner is trying to describe. And his sentence about learning 'to know the physical world purely through *itself* without adding one's own thoughts' brings to mind Nietzsche's triumphant cry: 'Pure will, without the troubles and perplexities of intellect! How happy! how free!'

What was happening was that Steiner was slowly ceasing to be the shy, shrinking, self-conscious young man, of whom Friedrich Eckstein said 'He didn't know a thing.' It had taken him a long time to grow up. During the first half of his life he had been a typical 'outsider' figure, withdrawn into a world of his own thoughts, looking at the real world as if he was looking through the glass of an aquarium. Now, at last, he was in contact with the real world, and felt no more need to retreat hastily back into the safety of his mental world.

'I was aware that I was experiencing an inner transformation of soul-life which normally occurs at a much earlier age.' And he came to the interesting conclusion that for most people, it happens too early. They emerge from the shy, inner world of the child and adolescent, and learn to come to terms with the real world around them. The result is that the two worlds mix, like hot and cold water, the result being lukewarm water. Because Steiner had taken so much longer to make contact with the external world, he had also acquired the knack of preventing the two from diluting one another.

It had happened at exactly the right time. Steiner's work in Weimar was drawing to a close; he had completed his edition of Goethe's scientific writings. And while no doubt he could have stayed on at the Goethe Archive indefinitely, he was experiencing the need to move on. The desire to express his convictions was becoming increasingly strong. 'My special concern at this period of my life was that ideas which I had to reject emphatically had taken such an intense hold upon thinking in general. These ideas were so universally accepted that people were unable to see the possibilities inherent in anything that opposed them.' And Steiner had to face the fact that his own books were doing nothing to change the opinions of the age. His highly abstract style guaranteed that very few people read them. Sooner or later, he would have to go out into the world and preach. But where would he begin? 'Thus at every turn I met the problem: How can I find the way to express in terms understandable to my contemporaries what I inwardly perceive directly as truth?' And it is significant that the following chapter of his Autobiography—Chapter 24—is the only one that bears a title: 'Must I remain silent?'

Steiner's thoroughly unpractical solution to the problem was to purchase a moribund magazine called *The Review of Literature*. It was unpractical, to begin with, because the magazine had only a few subscribers. A Frank Harris or a G. K. Chesterton might have turned it into a success; but Steiner was the last man in the world to improve its circulation. His brief editorship of the *German Weekly Review* in 1888 had shown that he had no talent in this direction. Worse still, the owner would only sell it if Steiner accepted as co-editor a pleasant but lazy man-about-town called Otto Erich Hartleben, an 'aesthete' who spent half his time in Italy and the other half in Berlin cafés. Steiner liked him—he seems to have liked everybody—but found it impossible to work with him.

Nevertheless, the magazine seemed to offer the only solution to the problem of how to reach a wider audience. So in July 1897, Steiner finally severed his connection with Weimar and became an editor in Berlin.

The change was not particularly pleasant. Once again, he found himself living in uncomfortable lodgings. The people he now associated with were friends of Hartleben and members of a group called the Independent Literary Society who regarded the magazine as their own platform. Steiner says mildly: 'Those who were connected with the *Review* . . . were not particularly serious-minded people. Only a very few had any deeper interests.' And it does not take a great deal of reading between the lines to see that they regarded Steiner as what would nowadays be called a 'nut'. With charming honesty, Steiner admits that Weimar friends had failed to understand his ideas, but had been willing to accept that he had something of value to contribute. This new circle, he says with obvious understatement, did not share that impression. So his first experience of attempting to reach the wider public must have been something of a disillusionment.

Steiner, fortunately, was not the kind of man to be discouraged by incomprehension. His 'spiritual insight' suggested that all this was 'the working of destiny', a healthy-minded attitude that protected him from the discouragement he would have certainly experienced as a younger man.

His permanent lack of money did nothing to ease the situation. The magazine staggered on from crisis to crisis, and caused endless anxiety. Steiner's own reviews and articles, far from increasing its circulation, alienated many subscribers, particularly a group associated with the University of Berlin. Once again, he was spending his time sitting around in cafés with impecunious writers, just as if the last ten years had never happened. Some of the writers—like the dramatist Frank Wedekind—were men of genius; but they still had nothing whatever in common with Steiner. 'My position became uncomfortable within this circle because I realized why I was there, but the others did not.' And why was he there? To fulfil his destiny, to speak openly of his knowledge of the spirit. It was a pity that no one seemed interested.

At least he was able to renew his acquaintance with the theatre. The magazine was also associated with an independent Drama Society', who hired theatres for matinée performances of uncommercial plays—such as Maeterlinck's symbolist drama *The Intruder*. Steiner introduced this play with a short lecture, and thoroughly enjoyed himself. Whether his audience did is another matter: 'it afforded opportunity to convey a mood of true spirituality'. Cultivated Berliners found Steiner's brand of spirituality incomprehensible. In this age of Freud and Ibsen, Strindberg and Wedekind, H. G. Wells and Bernard Shaw, his 'idealism' must have struck most of them as a stale leftover from the 1850s.

Not the least of his personal problems was the 'utter misery of living alone'. At least this improved when Anna Eunicke moved from Weimar to Berlin in 1898; she took a house in the suburb of Friedenau, and invited Steiner to become a lodger. But the daughters were now grown up, and the presence of this still fairly young man in a house full of women probably gave rise to gossip. For whatever reason, Steiner and Anna Eunicke were married on 31 October 1899.

For the short period it lasted, Steiner's marriage seems to have been a happy one. An interesting glimpse into his domestic life can be found in the memoir written by a working man named Alwin Rudolph, who called upon Steiner towards the end of 1898 as an emissary of the College of the Workers' Educational Association. The College was looking around for someone to undertake the thankless task of lecturing on history—the lectures were usually so dry that most of the students dropped out after a week or so, and the lecturers became discouraged. Someone suggested a certain poet, and the poet suggested Steiner. So a delegation led by Herr Rudolph called upon Steiner at the house in Friedenau.

They were shown into a large room with an enormous desk by a young woman—one of the daughters. There was an older woman in the room, as well as Rudolf Steiner, a small, slim man dressed in black, with an untrimmed moustache and a flowing bow tie. Steiner was friendly and welcoming, and in no time at all, pastries had been produced and a coffee grinder was at work on the table. Of the women, Rudolph says: 'Actually I ought not to speak of them as "ladies", because they were two simple women, open-minded and many sided.' Presumably he means to say that they did not strike him as at all 'upper class'—if anything, the reverse. They seemed to treat Steiner with reverence, and it never occurred to Rudolph that the older woman might be — or might become—Mrs Steiner.

Without hesitation, Steiner agreed to give the course of lectures. The working men were so overwhelmed by all the hospitality and friendliness that they even forgot to mention the question of money—the fee for the course was a mere eight marks. Accordingly, Rudolph was ordered to return and find out whether Dr Steiner would be insulted by such a small sum. His reception this time was even friendlier; Steiner greeted him by taking both hands. Once more, coffee was produced, and when Steiner told him it was heated by spirits, there was a certain amount of joking about the word. The daughter produced a rag doll of Dr Steiner, and lifted the black frock coat to reveal a bottle of brandy. The girl explained that 'his whole body is spirit'. Rudolph, a Marxian materialist, was a little bewildered by these jokes, but deeply impressed by Steiner—so much so that he again omitted to mention fees.

On 13 January 1899, Steiner arrived for his first lecture at two minutes to eight—it was due to begin at eight—once more accompanied by his two faithful females. The room was small, for the College was accustomed to the audience dwindling steadily during the ten-week course. The little man with the friendly face and Austrian accent lauched himself into the lecture, speaking without notes, and the crowded audience was deeply impressed. Some of them even said afterwards that he ought to be a Member of Parliament.

The situation was, of course, paradoxical. The Workers' Educational Association was founded on Marxian principles, so its view of history was totally materialistic. Steiner was not in the least bothered by this; in fact, he saw it as his task to convert them to his own views in the gentlest possible manner. We may regard his attitude as either pragmatic or

Machiavellian. He says: 'It must be remembered that there are partial truths in the materialistic ideas on economics . . . Had I simply ignored them and taught history from an idealistic point of view, the workers would have sensed that what I said was not in agreement with the partial truths they knew . . .'. In other words, Steiner allowed them to assume that he agreed with Marx's economic theory of history. But he immediately added a reservation. It was nonsense to speak of economic forces dominating history before the sixteenth century, because economic life did not take on a form that could be understood in a Marxian sense until that time. Any good Marxist would have told him indignantly that the sixteenth century was the age of mercantile capitalism, and was just as dominated by class conflict as the nineteenth century. Fortunately, Steiner's audience consisted of respectful workers who were overawed by his enormous erudition. So they raised no objections when Steiner explained that before the sixteenth century, the great human ideals were spiritual, and that only in recent centuries have these become weakened by materialism. Probably no one even guessed that Steiner was not an orthodox Marxist. 'It would have been useless to enter into a controversy about materialism; I had to let idealism arise out of materialism,' says Steiner cunningly.

Fortunately, he adds, the leaders of the workers were not in the least interested in the College, so he had a free hand. Besides, no one could afford to look a gift horse in the mouth; Steiner charged only eight marks, and his lectures remained crowded throughout the course. Soon, other workers wanted him to come and address them. Trade unions asked him to lecture on science: Haeckel's *Riddle of the Universe* was the current bestseller, and discussing this was a delicate task, since it was a passionate attack on all forms of religion. (Steiner solved this problem by telling his audience that only the biological part of the book was valid, and the rest ought to be destroyed.) For the Gutenberg anniversary, he was asked to address an audience of seven thousand in the Berlin circus.

But if Steiner was quite happy to consort with the enemy, the enemy was less broad-minded. Sooner or later, the leaders of the working-class movement in Berlin were bound to realize that they were nurturing a viper in their bosom.

One of them attended a lecture, and declared 'In the proletarian movement we do not want freedom—we want reasonable compulsion.' But Steiner's pupils remained loyal. His audience in the rented rooms in the Annenstrasse swelled from fifty or so to over two hundred; instead of lasting until eleven o'clock, his lectures usually went on until after midnight. And Steiner was in his element. At last he was addressing the 'masses', and discovering that, in spite of his somewhat abstract mode of expression, he was a charismatic orator. It took the leaders of the Berlin socialist movement another four years to dislodge him; and by that time, Steiner had moved on to an even more appreciative audience.

What excited Steiner's listeners so much was that they were asked to participate. The German method of teaching tends to be authoritarian; the audience listens quietly, then goes home. Steiner's friendly manner made it easy for his audience to ask questions and join in the discussion. The lesson he learned became the basis for Steiner's later educational theory. Nowadays we take it for granted that audiences join in the discussion after a lecture and that the aim of education is to encourage the student to develop his individuality. It is almost impossible to grasp how revolutionary these ideas seemed in Berlin in the last year of the nineteenth century.

Steiner was involved with other groups and societies beside the Workers' College. One of these was called 'die Kommenden', the Future Ones, and its central figure was the Jewish writer and social thinker Ludwig Jacobowski, who ran a magazine called *Society* and devoted his life to combating anti-semitism. In fact, Steiner went on to lecture to the Jacobowski group after his opening lecture at the Workers' College. When Jacobowski died of meningitis in 1900, at the age of thirty-two, Steiner gave his funeral oration.

Another group with whom Steiner soon became involved was the Giordano Bruno Union, a group of 'monistic idealists'— i.e. people who believe that the only basic reality is spirit. Steiner attended the opening lecture, given by his friend Bruno Wille in 1900 and demonstrated that, in the social sphere, he was still prone to ineptness. Wille lectured on Goethe's remark that there is no matter without spirit. Afterwards, Steiner commented that Goethe had supplemented these words with the important amplification that 'polarity and intensification are direct manifestations of the spirit at work in creation'. Understandably, Wille saw this as a form of one-upmanship—as Steiner would have realized if he had thought twice before speaking. But the friendship survived, and Steiner was later asked to teach history at a newly created Independent College launched by Wille and other 'Bruno-ites'.

Philosophically speaking, Steiner's friends—and critics—must have wondered whether he was coming or going. In Jacobowski's *Society* he published a spirited defence of Haeckel, whose *Riddle of the Universe* he had dismissed so cavalierly. In his *Review*, Steiner published articles by an anarchist friend, the Scot John Henry Mackay, who preached a non-violent social revolution. He was influenced by his liking for Mackay and the fact that Mackay had been best man at his marriage; but respectable readers of the *Review* were outraged that it should be turned into a platform for anarchism, and cancelled their subscriptions by the dozen. (The magazine was also banned in Russia.) Steiner's lectures at the Workers' College lent credibility to the view that he was a disguised fellow-traveller. Yet he infuriated the members of the Giordano Bruno Union with a lecture on 'monism' in which he praised Scholasticism, pointing out that thinkers like Duns Scotus and Thomas Aquinas were monists in the sense that they believed that the universe is basically spiritual in nature. His audience found it impossible to understand why Steiner should speak sympathetically of the Church that had burned Giordano Bruno, and suspected that he was trying to smuggle in Catholicism by the back door.

In spite of these controversies—and the steady decline of the magazine—Steiner's reputation was spreading by word of mouth. In 1900, a young member of the Berlin lodge of the Theosophical Society approached two of its leading members, Count and Countess Brockdorff, and suggested that Rudolf Steiner would be a suitable person to deliver a lecture on Nietzsche. He had been excited by a curious article Steiner had written about Goethe's 'Fairy Tale', which Steiner interpreted as an 'esoteric' parable about the supersensible world. On 22 August 1900 Steiner delivered a lecture on Nietzsche in the library of the Berlin Theosophical Society. It went down well. Steiner had forgotten about Theosophy since his brief flirtation with it in Vienna in the 1880s, although he had made some hostile comments about it in his magazine. Now he noticed that some people in the audience were 'people who had great interest in the world of spirit'. He was asked to come again. On 29 September 1900, he lectured on the 'secret revelation' of Goethe's 'Fairy Tale'. It was, in a sense, a historic occasion, for this was the first time that Steiner had ever spoken out publicly about his 'spiritual researches'.

The Theosophists asked for more. Steiner obliged with talks on two mystics, Meister Eckhart and Jacob Boehme, and followed them up with another twenty-three lectures on various aspects of mysticism and the inner life. One member of his audience told him one day that his ideas were not in accordance with those of Annie Besant, leader of the English branch of the Theosophical Society. Steiner replied mildly: 'Is that so?', and went on as before.

But most of the members, including Count and Countess Brockdorff, were less critical. They sensed that Steiner was speaking from some direct personal knowledge, and they were intrigued. So, apparently, was a rather attractive young woman who began to appear at the lectures—Marie von Sivers, who had been brought up in Russia, studied drama at Paris, and only recently had decided against making a career as an actress. She approached Steiner and asked him whether it was not time to launch a new spiritual movement in Europe. Steiner agreed that it was, and sensing—correctly—that she was asking whether he was willing to lead such a movement, replied that he would only be available to 'call into life' a movement linked to Western occultism. He meant, of course, that he was not interested in developing Madame Blavatsky's Eastern form of theosophy.

According to the biographer of Marie von Sivers,* it was this conversation that brought Steiner to a decision. 'After the decisive question had been put . . . it became possible for Rudolf Steiner to approach his task, to become a spiritual leader of mankind.'

*Marie Steiner-von Sivers, by Marie Savitch.

The meeting with Marie von Sivers marked the end of Steiner's marriage—although he and Anna were to live together until 1903—and the beginning of his career as a public personality.

Six

Occultist and Guru

THE rise of the Steiner movement in Europe between 1900 and 1910 was one of the most remarkable cultural phenomena of our time. It raises certain basic questions that must be examined before we proceed any further.

James Webb put the problem in a nutshell when he wrote: '[Steiner's] transition from liberal academic to mystical lecturer is at first sight baffling.' He goes on to explain that Steiner's work on Goethe had prepared the ground for his theosophical convictions. We have already seen that this is untrue; the gap between the Goethe scholar and the author of *Cosmic Memory* is so vast as to be unbridgeable in normal intellectual terms.

Steiner's enemies had an uncharitable but plausible explanation: that Steiner seized the opportunity presented to him by a gullible group of Theosophists to create a new 'religion' that would appeal to his contemporaries. Steiner's followers reply that, on the contrary, his convictions all sprang from inner experience, and that most of them had already formed before he became a Theosophist. Let us try to study both sides of the argument impartially.

The anti-Steiner case runs as follows. Before he began lecturing to the Theosophists, Steiner was known as a liberal academic who was opposed to the total materialism of Haeckel. Yet his views were so confused that he wrote a book defending Haeckel. In these same years—towards the turn of the century—he made many hostile remarks about Christianity. Yet by the autumn of 1901 he was lecturing to the Theosophists on 'Christianity as Mystical Fact', and apparently accepting Madame Blavatsky's cosmology of the 'seven root races' and the existence of Atlantis and Lemuria. As time went by, Steiner expanded his view of Christianity until it became the central event in human history; as a result he acquired a large following of Protestant clergymen. Towards the end of his life, he had actually created his own branch of the Protestant Church, the 'Christian Community'.

It must be admitted that there is a certain amount of supporting evidence for the 'opportunist' view. In the Autobiography, Steiner states that 'a conscious knowledge of true Christianity' began to dawn in him in the Berlin period, and that it grew deeper towards the turn of the century, culminating in a revelation when he stood 'in the spiritual presence of the Mystery of Golgotha in a most profound and solemn festival of knowledge'. According to the later Steiner, the 'Christ event' was the central event in human history. What happened, he said, was that a divine being, who had been preparing for incarnation since the beginning of human evolution, descended to earth in the last three years of the life of the historical Jesus and took over his body. His purpose was to turn the tide of battle against the forces of materialism (aided by 'evil' powers called Ahriman and Lucifer), which would otherwise have overwhelmed humankind. Further complications are added to this story by the fact that, according to Steiner, there were actually two historical Jesuses, one a descendant of kings and a reincarnation of the Persian prophet Zarathustra, and the other a 'simpleton' who had never before been reincarnated as a human being. They lived together in Nazareth at the same time. But the 'Zarathustra Jesus' died, and his mother took over the upbringing of the other Jesus. All this, according to Steiner, explains why there is such a discrepancy between the early chapters of the Gospels of Matthew and Luke: they were talking of two different Jesuses...

None of this, however, is to be found in the series of lectures Steiner delivered to the Theosophists in the winter of 1901–2, *Christianity as Mystical Fact*. Most of the book is devoted to an exposition of the 'ancient Mysteries', those secret rites and doctrines that contained the essence of the old religions. Those who were admitted to these secrets were the Initiates. The initiate knew that God 'slumbers' in nature. But the initiate knows that God is also to be found in his own soul, and that 'the soul is a sacred place where the spellbound god may wake to liberty'. The Father is the spellbound god, asleep in nature; the Son is the awakened God, born out of the human soul. All of this is, of course, perfectly in accordance with the doctrines Steiner has already enunciated in his books on Goethe and Nietzsche: man must awaken his hidden powers.

The lectures continued with a section on the Greek sages before Plato, the mysticism of Plato, the neo-Platonists, the Mystery wisdom of Egypt, and finally, Jesus as a representative of the Mystery religions, an Initiate.

There was nothing here that was likely to offend a Theosophist—after all, Madame Blavatsky had stated that all religions are different approaches to Truth, and that there is no religion higher than Truth. In fact, what Steiner had to say in *Christianity as Mystical Fact* bears a remarkable resemblance to a work that had been published in 1889, *The Great Initiates* by Edouard Schuré. Schuré, twenty years Steiner's senior, was a French dramatist and critic who, like Steiner, detested scientific materialism. *The Great Initiates*—an immediate bestseller—began with the sentence: 'The greatest evil of our time is the fact that science and religion appear as two hostile forces that cannot be reconciled with one another.' It goes on to speak about esoteric teaching: 'All great religions have an exterior and an interior history, one open to all, the other secret.' This secret religion, 'once seen, shines out, luminous and organic, always in harmony with itself. It might also be called the history of eternal, of universal religion.' And in the remainder of this large book, he sets out to show that various religious figures of the past—Rama, Krishna, Hermes, Moses, Orpheus, Pythagoras, Plato, and Jesus—were all 'great Initiates' of this one, universal religion. Much is made, of course, of Jesus's initiation into the mystery sect of the Essenes, and the 'esoteric instruction' he received. 'We are beginning to understand that Jesus at the very height of his consciousness, the transfigured Christ, is opening his loving arms to his brothers, the other Messiahs who preceded him, beams of the Living Word as he was, that he is opening them wide to Science in its entirety, Art in its divinity, and Life in its completeness.'

Marie von Sivers had been deeply influenced by Schuré, and became his translator. So it seems conceivable that it was she who introduced Steiner to *The Great Initiates*, and who was responsible for the view of 'Jesus the Initiate' that we find in *Christianity as Mystical Fact*.

In the Autobiography, Steiner defends himself against many of these criticisms and, if we can accept his basic premises, it must be admitted that his arguments are convincing. Steiner insisted that when a man has developed the power to withdraw 'inside himself'—through Imagination, Inspiration, and Intuition—he becomes aware of spiritual realities, and that these include the life history of the human race. He develops the power to read the 'Akashic records', the imperishable record of the past that is imprinted on the psychic ether. Madame Blavatsky also had this power, but she only achieved it in trance, when the 'hidden Masters' spoke through her. The result was that much of what she records in *Isis Unveiled* and *The Secret Doctrine* was only partly true. Steiner was able to perceive the 'spirit world' in full consciousness, and he insisted that his own revelations about the remote past were as accurate as he could make them.

In writing about Steiner's description of the 'etheric body', Anne Bancroft comments: 'It is here that we begin to pull back a little, if we are honest. For nobody except a clairvoyant has actually seen an etheric body.'* This is true; but then, there *is* a great deal of evidence for the existence of the etheric body or 'life field', not only in the testimony of hundreds of clairvoyants, but in the work of scientists like Harold Burr, who established the existence of this electrical 'life field' by attaching delicate voltmeters to living creatures. † We may choose to be intellectually convinced by such evidence, even if we have never actually seen a 'life field'. The same is true of the power of 'psychometry' (which I have discussed in Chapter 1.) There is extremely convincing evidence that certain people can 'read' the history of objects which they hold in their hands. Most of these people actually 'see' these past events, as if looking at a mental cinema screen.

Dowsing as we have seen, is another baffling faculty that eludes scientific explanation, although it has been extensively

---

Twentieth Century Mystics and Sages, p. 265.
† See *Blueprint for Immortality: The Electric Patterns of Life* by Harold Burr (1972) and my *Mysteries*, p. 388.

studied by science. A good dowser can 'tune in' to whatever he happens to be looking for, and ignore other things. He can, for example, locate copper coins hidden under a carpet, and ignore silver ones; then, a moment later, he can locate the silver coins and ignore the copper ones. It is as if some curious faculty of the mind could be brought into operation at will. There is a certain amount of evidence that this faculty may be connected with the right cerebral hemisphere.

So no one who has considered the overwhelming evidence for 'extra-sensory perception' will dismiss Steiner's claims out of hand. Moreover, no reader of the Autobiography or *The Philosophy of Freedom* is likely to conclude that Steiner was an intellectual charlatan. He makes an impression of rigid intellectual honesty.

This leaves us with a problem which looks in rational terms, basically insoluble. It would be simple if we could dismiss Steiner as an opportunist who adopted Theosophy because it offered him a platform, and deliberately formulated his views about Atlantis and the Christ Revelation as a mythology to satisfy the needs of his followers. But this would involve the assumption that the Dr Jekyll of *The Philosophy of Freedom* turned into the Mr Hyde of *Cosmic Memory* and *An Outline of Occult Science*, and this seems, to put it mildly, unlikely.

It might be more constructive to ask: does it really matter? And the answer is: probably not. An interesting parallel case is that of Gurdjieff, whose complex cosmology involves a hierarchy of 'higher worlds', and the belief that men are 'food for the moon'. But it is possible to regard Gurdjieff as one of the greatest teachers of the twentieth century without paying the slightest attention to his cosmology. The essence of Gurdjieff's teaching lies in his statement that men are victims of a form of mechanicalness which he calls 'sleep', and that with sufficient effort, we can wake up. In short, we may feel that Gurdjieff's greatest significance lies in his psychology, not his cosmology.

The same is certainly true for Rudolf Steiner. The essence of his thought lies in the recognition that human freedom plays an active part in perception (although we usually fail to notice this, except in rare 'orgasmic' experiences). Once this is recognized, says Steiner, it is possible to develop this 'faculty of freedom' by deliberate effort. The result, he says, is 'knowledge of higher worlds'. He insists that this knowledge involves glimpses of mental horizons that are at present inconceivable to us. The knowledge he details in *Cosmic Memory* brings most of us to what Renée Haynes has called 'the boggle threshold' fairly quickly. But deciding to reject it—or simply to regard it as 'unproven'—does not necessarily entail rejecting more 'testable' aspects of Steiner's philosophy. One of Steiner's leading commentators, Stewart Easton, remarks about Steiner's 'Christology': 'I had the overwhelming impression that even if much that Steiner had to say on other subjects might be mistaken or erroneous, he simply could not have been mistaken on the *cosmic* nature of Christ . . .'. What is interesting here is the admission that Steiner might often have been mistaken or erroneous. Steiner himself insists repeatedly that he does not wish to be taken on faith; everything he says should be tested. Presumably, therefore, he himself would recommend us to reject—or regard as unproven—anything that pushes us over the 'boggle threshold'.

How is it conceivable that Steiner could be mistaken or in error about various subjects? He himself provided the answer in recognizing the affinity between 'inner visions' and dreams. To 'relax into the right brain' is, to some extent, to enter a world of strange impressions and glimpses: that is, of intuitions. One of the greatest of Steiner's fellow visionaries, Emanuel Swedenborg, was undoubtedly a genuine clairvoyant; yet in one of his books he has detailed descriptions of the inhabitants of the planets that we now know to be absurd. William Denton's book *The Soul of Things** has many extraordinary 'psychometric' descriptions of Rome and Pompeii that have been proved to be accurate; but he also devotes a volume to descriptions of the planets that are as nonsensical as Swedenborg's. In this curious world of 'inner vision', there are no hard and fast rules for distinguishing between reality and fantasy. So where Steiner is concerned, we may accept whatever strikes us as demonstrably true, and reject the rest with a good conscience.

*See my *Psychic Detectives*, Chapter 2.

Before speaking of Steiner's cosmology, let us glance briefly at that of Madame Blavatsky, so we can observe their points of similarity. Madame Blavatsky's history of the human race is set out in *The Secret Doctrine*, which is largely a commentary on an ancient work that she calls The Book of Dzyan. (It is written in 'Senzar', the ancient language of the Initiates.) According to the Book of Dzyan, there was orginally a great nothingness, the night of Brahm, which ended when the vibrations of eternity announced the cosmic dawn. These vibrations split into seven rays, who became intelligent beings, Dhyan Chohans, who proceeded to create the universe from electricity. (Since the electron was not discovered until after her death, this was a fairly good guess.) The process of creation begins with diffused cosmic matter, then a fiery whirlwind, which leads to the creation of a vast nebula, or cloud of cosmic gas.

The earth, which condenses out of this gas, is destined to pass through seven periods, or Rounds; we are now in the fourth. During the first three Rounds, the earth was non-material; it hardened into matter only in the fourth Round.

The human race originated on earth hundreds of millions of years ago. It will also go through seven cycles (or root races): we are the fifth of these. The first race was purely spiritual in form, and inhabited an 'Imperishable Sacred Land' at some unstated location. The second race were Hyperboreans, who lived at a North Pole which was then a tropical region. These were also 'bodiless'. Procreation slowly developed towards the end of the second race, and continued into the third. It was in the midst of this third race period, about eighteen million years ago, that certain spiritual beings felt a longing to experience earthly existence, and descended to the physical plane; this was the 'Fall'. They possessed only three senses, hearing, touch, and sight. This race lived in a vast continent called Lemuria, in the Pacific Ocean. (Australia is a fragment of Lemuria; so is Easter Island.) Lemuria was destroyed by fire, and vanished into the ocean.

The fourth race were the Atlanteans, who lived on the fabulous continent in the midst of the Atlantic Ocean. In some respects, they were more highly developed than we are, and understood how to use electricity; they also invented powered flight. The early Atlanteans were giants, and were responsible for building the pyramids and structures like Stonehenge. But they misused their power and became black magicians, and their continent was finally destroyed in a watery cataclysm.

Our own root race is the fifth, and it began in northern Asia. Like all the other root races, it is divided into seven sub-races, and we are the fifth of these. The sixth is already beginning to form. Where matter is concerned, our race is the most 'solid' so far. This means that we are more 'entrapped' than any previous race. At the same time, we also have more possibilities of creative action than any previous race, just as a sculptor can work better in clay than in soft mud, and better in marble than in sandstone. In due course, we shall be replaced by a more etherialized sixth root race, and then by an almost purely spiritualized seventh . . .

The obvious objection to Madame Blavatsky's chronology is that it does not agree with that of modern archaeology and geology. In *The Secret Doctrine* she loses no opportunity of pointing out that science is still ignorant of many things. 'As regards the duration of the geological periods alone, the learned men of the Royal Society are all hopelessly at sea . . .'. But since the invention of carbon dating, we are in an altogether better position to state that the Great Pyramid was built a mere 2,500 years ago, not 75,000 years ago, and that the same goes for Stonehenge. The same techniques enable us to be reasonably certain about the history of mankind, and to state with a fair degree of certainty that a hundred thousand years ago (the date of some of the late Atlantean catastrophes) modern man (Cro-magnon) had not yet appeared upon the scene of history. It is true that there are still large areas of doubt—an American professor of history, Charles Hapgood, believes that 'maps of the ancient sea kings' suggest that there was a highly advanced civilization covering much of the globe in eight thousand BC, two thousand years before the first cities are supposed to have been built. But even this lends no support to Madame Blavatsky's vast epochs of ancient history.

From his earliest association with the Theosophical Society, Steiner insisted that he would never be willing to toe the party line; everything he taught would be drawn from his own direct knowledge and personal experience. The Theosophists accepted this, and in 1902 Steiner became secretary general of the German section with the approval of Annie Besant, who had succeeded Madame Blavatsky.

None of the books Steiner published in the first three years of his association with Theosophy are in any way contradictory of the views of Madame Blavatsky. *Mystics of the Dawn of the Modern Age* (the lectures on Eckhart, Boehme, etc), *From Buddha to Christ, Christianity as Mystical Fact*, and *Theosophy* were all perfectly acceptable to English as well as German Theosophists—in fact, the book on mystics was an immediate success and when Steiner visited London in 1903 a leading Theosophist told him that 'it contained the truth about Theosophy'.

In 1904, Steiner began to publish in the magazine he had started, *Lucifer-Gnosis*, chapters of a work called *From the Akashic Records* (translated as *Cosmic Memory*). And it is here, for the first time, that he attempts to go further than Madame Blavatsky, and contradicts her on many points. By comparing this with *The Secret Doctrine* we can see how far Steiner's cosmology diverged from that of Madame Blavatsky.

Steiner agrees with Madame Blavatsky that the earth had three previous 'incarnations', and he calls these (rather confusingly) Old Saturn, Old Sun, and Old Moon. Old Saturn was made of 'chaotic, undifferentiated substance', and was inhabited by creatures who were 'delicate, tenuous and ethereal', and who would later become human beings. Higher beings than man—whom Steiner calls 'hierarchies'—were in charge of this evolutionary process. It was through their interaction with the natural forces of Old Saturn that physical organs began to emerge. Man's physical body began to form in the Saturnian stage of evolution.

Then came a gap in time, when the 'seed' of man lay fallow, and the spiritual hierarchies built up their powers to further his evolution. The next earth—'Old Sun'—came into being. There was a still further 'hardening' of matter, and man acquired his second body, the 'etheric body' (or what we have referred to as the 'life field'). Man had reached the plant stage of evolution.

On the next earth—'Old Moon'—man was endowed with

the 'astral body'—the part of us that leaves the physical body during sleep, and in so-called 'out-of-the-body experiences'.

When man was finally reborn on our present earth, his body was still little more than a cloud of vapour. Here again, Steiner is fairly close to Madame Blavatsky. During its first two epochs, the human race remained 'ethereal'. The third epoch was the age of the Lemurians. These creatures communicated by telepathy, and had an intuitive understanding of plant and mineral life. A Lemurian could increase the strength of his arms at will, and lift enormous loads by using his will power. His intuition also placed him in direct contact with divine wisdom. The Lemurian women began to develop powers of imagination, and because this led them to enjoy certain things and dislike others, the first ideas of good and evil arose. It was during this Lemurian epoch that the moon split off from the earth, in order to give man a better chance to evolve—the 'moon forces' were causing man to 'condense' too quickly. (Moon rock brought back to earth from the first moon landing seems to suggest that Steiner was mistaken about this: scientists now believe that the moon was never a part of our earth, but was probably 'captured' from space.)

As he continues to 'harden', man becomes subject to certain evil or hostile forces, known as the Luciferic hierarchies. This is a point that requires some explanation. According to Steiner, it was the Divine intention that man should have free will. So—for some unexplained reason—the 'hierarchies' were first of all given a chance to exercise free will, and thus to rebel against God. Two different types of spiritual being took advantage of their freedom to rebel against the divine will; these Steiner refers to as the Luciferic and Ahrimanic beings. (These are called—for short—Lucifer and Ahriman.) Lucifer tempts man to pride, while Ahriman tries to push him to advance much faster than he should—for example, by scientific invention. Man is continually surrounded by these 'bad angels', who seize every opportunity to influence him.

Fear, illness, and death enter human history during the Lemurian period, due to the influence of the Luciferic beings. Man also develops a taste for rebellion through their influence. The result was an upsurge of egoism that led to a tremendous catastrophe, which put an end to Lemuria.

In the next epoch—Atlantis—man becomes more 'solid' still. These descendants of the Lemurians were unable to reason, but they possessed an abnormally powerful memory. They could control the life force in plants and use it as modern man uses coal. But Ahriman pushed them into merely scientific achievement, and even Initiates among them gradually became corrupt. Various sub-races hardened into egoism and power-seeking. Man became increasingly a slave of matter. Evil began to spread, and 'since the forces of growth and generation, if torn from their original sphere and used independently, have a mysterious connection with certain forces working in air and water, there were thus unchained, through human action, mighty destructive natural forces which led to the gradual ruin of Atlantean territory . . . '. Atlantis vanished as recently as 10,000 years ago, according to Steiner.

Our own age, the fifth epoch, is the post-Atlantean era. We are the fifth sub-race of this epoch. The first sub-race was Hindu, and their era began in 7227 BC. But they regarded the material world as illusion—'maya'—and so merely turned their backs on it. The second sub-race, the Persians, began in 5067 BC and ended in 2907; they regarded life as a crude battle between the forces of good and evil—Ahriman and Ahura Mazda. Next came the Egypto-Chaldeans, who discovered astrology, and who came altogether closer to accepting matter. Their age ended in 747 BC, the date of the founding of Rome. The Romans went further than any human beings so far in accepting the material world as the only reality—they even worshipped their emperors as gods. At this point in his evolution, man came close to being overwhelmed and permanently defeated by evil forces. And it was at this point that the 'hierarchy' called Christ descended into the body of Jesus of Nazareth—in the last three years of his life—and turned the tide of battle. Christ had been around since the beginning, and had been active on behalf of evolving humanity. By the time our earth was created, Christ had become the highest of the sun spirits, and the chief opponent of Lucifer. He realized that, at some point, he would have to enter a human body to finally set limits to the powers of Lucifer and Ahriman. His purpose was to launch a new stage of evolution, in which man finally established a conscious ego, an 'I', which could make its own choices, and whose evolution would be purely in its own hands. Steiner called this 'I' the 'intellectual soul'. The age of the intellectual soul came to an end in AD 1413, and was replaced by the age of the 'consciousness soul', in which we are still living. The consciousness soul has greater powers of objectivity than any previous soul; it can withdraw itself totally from the object of its studies. The age of the consciousness soul is also the age of the 'loner', the 'outsider'; in the previous age, human beings were far more conscious of being members of a group than of being individuals. The characteristic 'Mysteries' of this new age were those of the Rosicrucians, and Steiner seems to associate these with that widespread obsession of the Middle Ages, alchemy. 'Man prepared himself for his experiments as if for a sacred rite,' he says in *Mystery Knowledge and Mystery Centres*. Yet this experimental spirit in itself gradually led to our 'God estranged' civilization. According to Steiner, the *zeitgeist* ('spirit of the age') is a real entity, a guiding spirit whose purpose is to guide evolution in a particular epoch. During the 'Rosicrucian' epoch, this spirit of the age was the Archangel Gabriel, whose business was to lead the human spirit into materialism, to foster a healthy spirit of scepticism and experimentalism. In 1879 (the year Steiner went to Vienna), Gabriel gave way to the Archangel Michael, whose evolutionary task (as summarized by Stewart Easton) is 'to bring men together as individuals, so that they recognize their common humanity and Christ who lives within each human being'. Meanwhile, Steiner sees his own task as the inauguration of this new age: what has been lost through the descent into materialism can only be replaced by the new Mystery knowledge that he has given to mankind. Man must regain his perception of nature as 'God's living garment'. So Steiner sees himself as an important port of the world historical process. And there can be little doubt that when, in 1902, he became general secretary of the Theosophical Society, he hoped that he might succeed where Madame Blavatsky had failed, and create a new religion, a great spiritual movement that would finally rescue man from the consequence of materialism. The fountainhead of this new religion would be a Mystery centre, at the heart of which there would be a sacred temple . . . .

For the reader who is approaching Steiner for the first time, the last few pages must have raised many doubts. It is surely inconceivable—to put it bluntly—that he could have believed this preposterous rigmarole about Old Saturn and Lemuria and Atlantis?

It is reassuring to discover that Steiner was himself fully aware of these objections. He speaks of them in one of the lectures in *Karmic Relationships* (Vol. 6, No. 8), quoting the Belgian writer Maurice Maeterlinck. In *The Great Secret*, Maeterlinck says of Steiner: 'When he does not lose himself in visions—plausible, perhaps, but incapable of verification—of the prehistoric ages, and in the astral jargon concerning life on other planets, [he] is a clear and shrewd thinker . . .'. And he goes on:

> Steiner has applied his intuitive methods, which amount to a kind of transcendental psychometry, in order to reconstruct the history of the Atlanteans and to reveal to us what takes place on the sun, the moon and in other worlds. He describes the successive transformations of the entities which become men, and he does so with such assurance that we ask ourselves, having followed him with interest through the introductions which reveal an extremely well-balanced, logical and comprehensive mind, if he has suddenly gone mad or we are dealing with a hoaxer or with a genuine seer.

Maeterlinck's expression of the conundrum could hardly be improved. Steiner *is* a clear and shrewd thinker, and his insights are often profound. He is certainly no fake in the intellectual sense—no second-rate mind uttering pseudo-profundities. And it is quite plain that he has not gone mad. Is it conceivable that he is a kind of hoaxer—that is, that he has set out deliberately to create a religion for the twentieth century, and has recognized that such a religion needs a mythology, which he sets out to provide?

This explanation, which seems the most rational explanation of works like *Cosmic Memory*, becomes rather less convincing as one reads Steiner's later works, written (or delivered as lectures) long after he had broken with the Theosophical

Society. *Karmic Relationships,* a series of lectures delivered in 1924, runs to over a thousand pages, and it is only necessary to read the first dozen to realize that he is perfectly sincere. Besides, no man would elaborate a lie or a hoax at such length.

Was he, then, a genuine seer? That he was a seer there can be no doubt whatever. But does this mean that his 'visions' were invariably true? Here, unfortunately, the answer has to be negative. On Sunday 16 August 1924, Steiner visited 'King Arthur's Castle' at Tintagel, in Cornwall. It deeply impressed him, and in a lecture the following Friday in Torquay, he spoke at some length about the 'spiritual perceptions' he had gained as he gazed down from the ruins across the sea. 'From the accounts contained in historical documents', he explained to his audience,

> it will not be easy to form a true conception of the tasks and the mission of King Arthur and his Round Table . . . But this becomes possible when one stands on the actual site of the castle and gazes with the eye of the spirit over the stretch of sea . . . There, in a comparatively short space of time, one can perceive a wonderful interplay between the light and the air, but also between the elemental spirits living in light and air. One can see spirit-beings streaming to the earth in the rays of the Sun, one can see them mirrored in the glittering raindrops, one can see that which comes under the sway of earthly gravity appearing in the air as the denser spirit-beings of the air. Again, when the rain ceases, and the rays of the Sun stream through the clear air, one perceives the elemental spirits intermingling in quite a different way. There one witnesses how the sun works in earthly substance—and seeing it all from a place such as this, one is filled with a kind of pagan 'piety'—not Christian but pagan piety, which is something altogether different. Pagan piety is a surrender of heart and feeling to the manifold spiritual beings working in the processes of nature.

One can see that Steiner was greatly moved as he stood among the ruins where Arnold Bax had earlier written his famous tone poem *Tintagel.* He goes on to explain that to 'take hold of the spirit-forces working there' at Tintagel would have been beyond the power of one man; a group of men was necessary, one of whom felt himself to be the representative of the Sun (which, in Steiner, is always associated with Christ).

> It was here that King Arthur and his Twelve Knights drew into themselves from the Sun the strength wherewith to set forth on their mighty expeditions through Europe in order to battle with the wild, demonic powers of old, still dominating large masses of the population, and drive them out of men. Under the guidance of Arthur these men were battling for outer civilization.

He continues at some length, explaining that 'the whole configuration of this castle at Tintagel indicates that the Twelve under the direction of King Arthur were essentially a Michael-community . . .'.

In fact, archaeological evidence has revealed that in the time of King Arthur, the only building on the present site of Tintagel Castle was a Celtic monastery. The castle was built six hundred years later, around AD 1140, probably by Reginald, Earl of Cornwall, a bastard son of King Henry the First (who was, in turn, the son of William the Conqueror).

'King' Arthur was, in fact, a Roman general named Artorius, protégé of a commander called Ambrosius. When the Romans left England, about AD 410, Saxon mercenaries began to push back the original inhabitants—the Celts—towards the west and north. Arthur (probably born about AD 470) was the commander who defeated the Saxons again and again, and finally turned the tide in the battle of Badon, about AD 515. Unfortunately, the Celts, who had united magnificently against the Saxon invader, began to squabble amongst themselves, and Arthur spent the rest of his life trying to avoid being stabbed in the back by his own allies and relatives. He was mortally wounded in the battle of Camlann, around 540, fighting against his own nephew, and his body was almost certainly buried in Glastonbury Abbey, where it was discovered in May 1154 by monks digging a grave.

There can be very little doubt that Arthur never left England. His exploits as a conqueror of Norway and Gaul were invented by a Welsh ecclesiastic called Geoffrey of Monmouth in his *History of the Kings of Britain*, which dates from about 1135. According to Geoffrey, Arthur was marching on Rome when he was recalled to England by the rebellion of his nephew Mordred. In Geoffrey's account, King Arthur was born in Tintagel castle after the magician Merlin had metamorphosed King Uther Pendragon, so that he resembled the husband of a queen called Ygerne, with whom Uther was in love; Uther spent the night with her and she conceived Arthur. Merlin was invented by Geoffrey of Monmouth, although he may have been based on a northern bard called Myrddin. When Geoffrey was writing his *History* in the 1130s, there was no castle at Tintagel, although there were the ruins of a Celtic monastery. But a castle *was* built by the time the second edition of the book appeared in 1145 and it seems probable that Geoffrey saw it. (The first edition has vanished, so there is no way of knowing whether Tintagel Castle was mentioned in it as Arthur's birthplace.)

All this leaves no possible doubt that Steiner's 'spiritual perception' of King Arthur and his twelve Knights of the Round Table was pure imagination. (Geoffrey makes no mention of the Round Table; this was added by the Norman poet Wace in a long poem in 1155.) Steiner repeats his claim to have 'seen' the truth about King Arthur in another lecture in *Karmic Relationships* (Vol. 4, No. 4):

> Even today, if one is receptive to these things, one receives a very real impression which tells one what it was that the Knights of the Round Table of King Arthur did in their gigantic castle . . . Looking with occult vision at what takes place there to this day, we receive a magnificent impression. We see them standing there, these Knights of the Round Table, watching the play of powers of light and air, water and earth, the elemental spirits . . . It was the task of the Order of King Arthur, founded in that region by the instructions of Merlin, to cultivate and civilize Europe at a time when all Europe in its spiritual life stood under the influence of the strangest elemental beings . . . There were, so to speak, later 'campaigns of Alexander' undertaken by the Knights of the Round Table into Europe, even as the real campaigns of Alexander had gone from Macedonia into Asia.

The reference to Alexander the Great is explained in an earlier lecture, in which Steiner speaks of 'that genuine spiritual life which had been cultivated as between Aristotle and Alexander'. According to Steiner, the motive of Alexander in 'conquering the world' was to spread the treasures of wisdom far and wide. Although it is true that Alexander imbibed Greek culture from his teacher Aristotle, it is difficult for anyone who has studied his life to accept that he was interested in spreading the treasures of wisdom far and wide. He was an alcoholic who killed his best friend in a drunken rage, and his motives seem to have been typical of the 'world conqueror'—enjoyment of war for its own sake. Again, one suspects that Steiner was inventing another myth that was pleasing to his imagination.

In the lecture already cited, Steiner pokes mild fun at Maeterlinck. Maeterlinck had described him as 'one of the most erudite and also one of the most confusing among contemporary occultists'. This, says Steiner, is like saying that a man is both black and white at the same time. The comment is unfair; in fact, it is nonsensical. Maeterlinck is right: Steiner *is* both erudite and confusing, and there is no contradiction. Steiner shows the same weakness in argument when he derides the comment that the introductions to his books reveal a well-balanced mind, but that later pages make it seem that he has suddenly gone mad.

> Very well, then . . . I write a book. Maeterlinck reads the introduction and I seem to him to have an 'extremely well-balanced, logical and comprehensive mind'. Then he reads on, and I turn into someone who makes him say: I don't know whether Rudolf Steiner has suddenly gone mad, or whether he is a hoaxer or a seer. Then it happens again. I write a second book; when he reads the introduction Maeterlinck again accepts me as having an 'extremely well-balanced, logical and comprehensive mind' [Steiner obviously enjoyed repeating this phrase]. Then he reads further contents and again does not know whether I am a lunatic or a hoaxer or a seer. And so it goes on. But suppose everybody were to say: when I read your books you seem at the beginning, to be very clever, balanced and logical, but then you suddenly go mad! People who are logical when they begin to write and then as they write on suddenly become crazy, must indeed be extraordinary creatures! In the next book they switch round, are logical at the beginning and later on again lunatics!

But this kind of mockery leaves Maeterlinck's main point untouched. And the King Arthur episode suggests that he was basically correct. Steiner's 'occult vision' *could* be misled by his imagination. And once we know this, it becomes very difficult to accept Steiner's repeated assertions that his readings from the 'Akashic records' are 'a matter of conscientious research, no less exact in its methods than any researches in physics or chemistry . . .' (Vol. 4, p. 30). He tells us, for example, about how a certain Egyptian Initiate, whose business was embalming mummies, gradually lost interest in his work, and allowed a servant to do it for him. In a later existence, the Initiate was reborn as Julia, the nymphomaniac daughter of Augustus, who married Tiberius, while the servant became the Roman historian Livy. Later still, the servant was reborn as the medieval minstrel poet, Walter von der Vogelweide. The Initiate was reborn as a Tyrolese landowner who was Walter's patron. This landowner rediscovered the legendary castle of the Dwarf King Laurin, hollowed out of the rocks, which 'made a profound impression upon him'. Finally, he was reborn as August Strindberg, whose misogyny was a reflection of his unsatisfactory career as a Roman nymphomaniac, while the servant became Strindberg's friend Dr Ludwig Schleich. (It often happens, Steiner says, that people associated together in one existence meet again in later ones—for their karmas are interlinked.) Steiner met Schleich, and was able to trace back his previous lives by what Maeterlinck calls a kind of 'transcendental psychometry'.

Karmic Relationships is full of astonishing revelations of this sort. We learn that in an earlier existence, Karl Marx was a warlike Frenchman who often went off plundering his neighbours. One day he came back and found that his own house and lands had been seized by another noble; he was forced to become this noble's vassal. In due course, the two were reborn as Marx and Engels; Marx's bitterness at having his lands seized would seem to explain how he came to write *Das Kapital* . . .

Reflecting upon Eduard von Hartmann's afflicted knee— which compelled him to spend most of his life on a couch— Steiner tells how he was 'guided to one of his earlier incarnations' in which he was a knight in the Crusades. One day he met a man 'concerning whom he felt instinctively that he had had something to do with him in a still earlier life'. Moved by some instinctive distaste, Hartmann proceeded to persecute his former acquaintance in the midday sun. This injustice literally rebounded on Hartmann's head, for he suffered sunstroke. And because of some psychic law that connects the head and the knee, the sunstroke reappears in his later existence as a diseased knee . . .

In the same lecture, Steiner retells the story of his encounter with Nietzsche, and says he felt that Nietzsche's astral body and his ego were trying to escape, but his physical body and etheric body were too strong and healthy to allow this to happen. Steiner's spiritual vision then led him to Nietzsche's previous incarnation, as a Franciscan monk, who spent his days inflicting self-punishment, kneeling in front of the altar until his knees were a mass of bruises. This pain had the effect of knitting him closely with his physical body, so in his next incarnation, as Nietzsche, he had no desire to be in the body at all . . .

Steiner was obviously unaware of what now seems reasonably certain: that Nietzsche was suffering from the tertiary stage of syphilis. It is true that there are still some vestiges of doubt about this; but there can be no doubt that Nietzsche's illness was basically physical in origin, and not—as Steiner believed—simply the result of his detestation of the age he was born into. Again, one is inclined to entertain some mild doubts about Steiner's 'spiritual vision'.

The answer to this central problem about Steiner can be found in his own writings about the 'spiritual world'. In 1912 and 1913 he produced two little books—now usually published together—called A Road to Self-Knowledge and The Threshold of the Spiritual World. They contain an extremely useful and lucid summary of his ideas on man's 'four bodies', on 'supersensible worlds', on 'cosmic beings', and so on. Discussing how 'spiritual events' and beings come to manifest themselves, he compares it to the act of remembering something. 'Now let us imagine an image rising up in the soul in the same way as a picture of memory, yet expressing not something previously experienced, but something unfamiliar . . . If we do this, we have formed an idea of the way in which the spiritual world first makes its appearance in the soul when the latter is sufficiently prepared for it.' And he explains: 'If the soul wishes to acquire the ability to enter knowingly into the supersensible world, it must first of all strengthen its powers by unfolding from within an activity which is fundamentally one of imagining.'

To sceptics, this sounds like an admission that Steiner's 'visions' were pure imagination. But anyone with the slightest acquaintance with the occult tradition will read quite a different meaning into it. We have already noted Aldous Huxley's comment that man has an immense inner world that could be compared to the earthly globe. Occultists call this the 'astral world'. We can, according to the magical tradition, learn to 'travel' in this world just as in the physical world. What it requires basically is a highly developed power of *visualization*. This involves training oneself to summon up mental pictures that are as clear as real objects—for example, one of the simplest exercises is imagining a wooden cube, and trying to visualize it so clearly that you can turn it around, look at it from every angle, feel the texture of the wood, even smell it. Eventually it should even be possible to visualize with the eyes open, projecting the image into the real world. One authority on the subject suggests that it should take about a month of practice, for a quarter of an hour each day.*

Once this has been achieved, the next stage is to make a series of five cards containing 'tattwa symbols'—symbols for earth, air, fire, water, and ether; the symbols are coloured respectively yellow, blue, red, silver, and black. A symbol should be chosen, and then stared at until it produces an 'after image'; this after image will be in its complementary colour. At this point, the symbol should be visualized in its complementary colour, with the eyes closed. It should then be regarded as a *doorway*, and the next step is to try to pass—imaginatively—through this doorway. This is the first step of 'astral travel.' Depending on what symbol has been chosen, the 'landscape' on the other side of the doorway should be

*J. H. Brennan, *Astral Doorways* (Aquarian Press, 1971).

quite distinctive. And, according to practised 'astral voyagers', it can be explored like any other landscape.

Most of us will, admittedly, find it very difficult to envisage any such result, for our powers of visualization are feeble. There is, nevertheless, nothing 'unscientific' about the notion. The psychologist Jung called it 'active imagination', and had no doubt that it was a faculty that could be developed by most people—although he warned about the danger of developing these powers without proper supervision. In his autobiography, Jung describes how he came to discover his own power of active imagination. After the break with Freud in 1912, Jung went through a mental crisis, and was for a time afraid of losing his sanity. Life became a continual struggle to fight off panic and foreboding. One day, seated at his desk, he suddenly decided to try the experiment of 'letting go' and surrendering completely to the chaotic forces of his unconscious mind. 'Then I let myself drop. Suddenly it was as though the ground literally gave way beneath my feet, and I plunged into dark depths.' Then he had a feeling of landing on a soft, sticky mass, and found himself in deep twilight. In a wholly real 'waking dream' he entered an underground cave and saw the body of a blond youth floating down a stream, with a red sun rising in the background.

Jung had discovered that he could 'dream' while awake, and he began to make regular voyages into these mental realms. On one of these 'journeys' he met an old man and a blind girl who seemed to be real people. Subsequently, holding conversations with one of these dream figures, he was convinced that 'it was he who spoke, not I'. It was this dream figure—whom he called Philemon—who taught him 'the objectivity of the psychic world'—a phrase of which Steiner would certainly have approved.

Like Ramakrishna after his attempt at suicide, Jung had induced in himself a permanent ability to enter these mental states, to break down inner barriers between the conscious and the unconscious.

Some people, like the mystic William Blake, seem to be born with the ability to enter this mental—or astral—world of visions; as a child, Blake was beaten for saying that he had seen a tree full of angels. But he undoubtedly *had* seen a tree full of angels. Blake also laid enormous stress on the idea of imagination, and emphasized that it is the gateway to inner worlds. Emanuel Swedenborg, whose temperament was altogether closer to Steiner's (he was trained as a scientist and engineer), had to pass through a severe mental crisis in middle life before he suddenly achieved his ability to see 'visions'.

Now we know that Steiner passed through a long period of mental crisis after he left Weimar—although he says so little about it in his autobiography that it is difficult to grasp exactly what happened. He says that his experience of Christianity 'underwent a severe test', and speaks of 'severe inner struggles during the time of testing': 'These inner struggles took place behind the scenes of everyday experience.' They resulted eventually in his 'revelation', when he stood 'in the spiritual presence of the Mystery of Golgotha in a most profound and solemn festival of knowledge'.

It is surely significant that this vision occurred just before the beginning of the new century, and of the new epoch in Steiner's life. Before this, he had been vaguely hostile to Christianity, feeling, like Nietzsche, that it was an excuse for indulging in daydreams of salvation. After the 'vision', Christ became the centre of Steiner's life. The 'vision' was Steiner's equivalent of Ramakrishna's experience of the Divine Mother; it is clear from his work that from then on the thought of Christ could produce a state of ecstasy, an immense welling-up of inner conviction. It was at this point that Steiner's philosophy became a 'Christology', with its central emphasis on Christ's descent into history to ensure man's ultimate salvation. This deep, unwavering conviction was the source of the enormous charisma that Steiner developed during this period of his life, and explains why his lectures made so many converts.

Steiner himself admits, in The Threshold of the Spiritual World, that 'it should on no account be denied that it is difficult to distinguish between illusions and realities in this sphere' of the spirit. He adds: 'Many people who believe they have manifestations from a spiritual world are certainly only occupied with their own memories, which they do not recognize as such.' He seems quite confident that he himself never makes this mistake. But, as we have seen in the case of his visit to Tintagel, he *was* capable of mistaking 'active imagination' for a perception of reality.

This is not to suggest that most of Steiner's 'spiritual perceptions' were a form of wishful thinking. Even a little book like *The Threshold of the Spiritual World* has a tone of sober precision, of scientific exactitude, that gives the reader an immediate sense of being in the hands of a man who knows what he is talking about. But when we turn from this to a book like *Cosmic Memory*, it is quite clear that the best attitude to Steiner is not one of unquestioning acceptance. Steiner *was* capable of being misled by his own highly developed powers of active imagination, and it is up to the individual reader to decide for himself just where he will draw the line. And since Steiner himself advises us never to accept what he says on trust, such an attitude can only increase those powers of scientific discernment and penetration that he regards as the foundation of 'spiritual vision'.

Seven

The Building of the Temple

IN July 1902, Steiner travelled to London with Marie von Sivers to attend a congress of the Theosophical Society. He wrote: 'At this Congress . . . it was already taken for granted that a German Section of the Society should be established, with me as the General Secretary.' So far there had only been a Theosophical 'lodge' in Berlin. Marie von Sivers had been working in Bologna, helping a Russian Theosophist to establish an Italian lodge of the Society. So both must have been regarded as figures of some importance. Steiner was to be not only the head of the German branch, but also of the movement in Switzerland and Austria-Hungary. His working-class friend Rudolph found him much changed when he returned to Berlin. He had shaved off his moustache and wore a bowler hat. He seemed to place a distance between himself and his students, and Rudolph says 'The intimacy we experienced with him before was never recovered.'

It was on 8 October 1902 that Rudolph attended a lecture by Steiner at the Giordano Bruno Bund, and it confirmed his worst fears. Instead of looking at his audience, Steiner stared out over their heads. His subject was 'Monism and Theosophy', and he began with an attack on Spiritualism. Then he went on to insist that any serious philosophy of life must be based on the scientific method. The trouble with modern science was that it was too narrow, and this resulted in materialism. But the real task of philosophy was to rise above materialism, to transform itself into theosophy by introducing the idea of God. He went on to speak approvingly of Thomas Aquinas as an example of a scientific 'monist', a man who based his life's work on reason, yet who recognized that God stands above reason.

Long before the lecture ended, it was obvious that Steiner and his audience were at loggerheads. When he finished, no one clapped and no one proposed a vote of thanks; the meeting broke up in silence. Rudolph broke with Steiner after this lecture.

Ten days later, Annie Besant was present when Steiner was appointed General Secretary of the German section of the Society. Ten days later still, he began a series of lectures to the new German Theosophical Society with a talk entitled 'Reflections on Karma'.

Steiner's own account of his life—in the Autobiography—ends in 1907; but the years from 1900 to 1907 occupy less than twenty-five pages, and are little more than a hotch-potch; when he wrote them, Steiner was already suffering from the abdominal illness that was to kill him. But the story was taken up by Steiner's secretary Guenther Wachsmuth in his monumental *Life and Work of Rudolf Steiner*, covering the period from 1900 to Steiner's death. Anyone who opens this book expecting a Boswellian account of Steiner will be disappointed. It seems to consist very largely of sentences like: 'After a brief lecture tour in South Germany, he went to Switzerland, and there, on September 19 in Basel, a new Group was inaugurated . . .'; 'In May 1907 he gave two public lectures in Munich on *The Bible and Wisdom*, followed by a cycle of fourteen lectures on *The Theosophy of the Rosicrucians . . .*'. In fact, Steiner's life between 1900 and 1925 is basically a record of his travels and his lectures. In twenty-five years he delivered over six thousand lectures—an average of one lecture for every single weekday. There were periods when this lecuring activity seemed to rise to a frenzy, as during the period of two and a half weeks in 1924 when he delivered seventy lectures.

By 1904, life was already becoming hectic. He had launched a magazine called *Lucifer*, and his correspondence was demanding. Wachsmuth records that a 'small group of persons' came together to try to smooth his path by their unselfish co-operation. They carried his outgoing mail down to the post office in laundry baskets.

The year 1904 also saw publication of the first of Steiner's major 'occult' works, *Theosophy—An Introduction to the Super-*

sensible Knowledge of the World and the Destination of Man. In the
opening chapter he explains that man is a threefold being,
consisting of body, soul, and spirit—not a twofold being,
consisting of body and soul, as Christianity has always taught.
Body is wholly material; spirit is wholly 'immaterial'. Soul is
the bridge between them, the part of man whose business is
to acquire and digest experience for the spirit—it might be
regarded as a kind of spiritual stomach. Man acquires a
different soul with every incarnation. Steiner's final arrange-
ment of the components of a human being is as follows: (1)
Physical body, (2) Etheric body (or Life-body), (3) Astral
body, (4) Ego, (5) Spirit self (which is the transmuted astral
body), (6) Life spirit (the transmuted etheric body), and (7)
Spirit man (the transmuted physical body). To link this with
Madame Blavatsky's Theosophy, Steiner also gives these
components their Hindu names.

The book continues with a brief account of reincarnation
and karma—the thread of 'acquired destiny' that runs from
life to life as man is reborn. Then there is an account of the
three worlds: physical, soul-world, and spirit-world, including
a section on what happens to man after death. The 'life field'
or etheric body dissolves in about three days, during which
time the ego and astral body see the whole of their past life
unfolding before them (just as people on the point of death
are supposed to see their past lives in a few seconds). Then
the ego and astral body enter purgatory (or 'kamaloca'), for a
period lasting about one third of the lifetime just completed,
during which the life is relived and re-evaluated. It could be
regarded as the equivalent of going through exam papers
with the teacher after an exam is over. Since the astral body is
still capable of feelings, it will suffer from all the unsatisfied
desires and lusts that it still contains. Finally, purified by this
suffering, the astral body can dissolve. In kamaloca, we also
experience everything we have done during our lives *seen
from the point of view of those to whom we have done it*. So the
murderer would experience his crime from the point of view
of the victim.

After kamaloca, the ego rises to the spirit world, and can
now choose its next life—and how to make restitution for any
wrongs committed in the previous one. We choose the

destiny we shall live through, the body we shall inhabit, as well as our parents and the people we shall know in the next life on earth; we often choose to associate once again with people we have known in previous lives, and whose destinies are interwoven with our own. It is, says Steiner, pointless to bemoan one's lot, because we have chosen it ourselves before being born.

Why, in that case, does everyone not choose to be handsome, rich, and successful? Because the spirit's aim is its own evolution, and good fortune and success could have the opposite effect. Spiritual progress can only be made on earth, not in the spirit world.

Theosophy concludes with a chapter on 'The Path of Knowledge', attempting to describe how a man can begin to acquire supersensible knowledge. Mathematics, he says, forms an excellent preparation for the Path, for it teaches logic, detachment, and concentration upon non-physical realities. In other words, the first requirement for the 'seeker' is the scientific attitude, the certainty that the mind *can* create order out of chaos. Man is not the helpless plaything of external forces, no matter how powerful and bewildering these forces may be. The first step is to recognize that he is capable of detachment, of using his mind as a compass to navigate his way through the confusion. Once he has done this, he has already taken the first step towards 'spiritual perception'. He will never again surrender totally to a sense of meaninglessness or defeat, for he knows that his real being is rooted in the eternal world.

Of all Steiner's books, *Theosophy* is probably the best through which to approach Steiner's ideas. It is short and well written (which is more than can be said for its successor, *Knowledge of the Higher Worlds and Its Attainment*, which is dry and abstract). It states his basic views about the spirit and life after death clearly and straightforwardly. But even if we choose to reject these—or to suspend judgement on them— the book has an *atmosphere* of serenity and detachment that produces on the reader the same effect as the *Bhagavad Gita*, or the Meditations of Marcus Aurelius, or Boethius' *Consolations of Philosophy*. It allows the open-minded reader to take the measure of Steiner's mind; and no matter what doubts we may feel about his 'esoteric' doctrines, that measure is impressive. No book shows more clearly that, no matter what his faults may have been, Steiner was no charlatan.

Yet for anyone with a wider interest in the 'paranormal', the book *does* raise some puzzling questions. Steiner's attitude to spiritualism seems to be one of complete dismissal. On the day after the notorious 'Monism' lecture he told a disciple that 'the spiritualists are the worst materialists of all'. In the light of his own philosophy, it is easy to understand why he said this: there *is* a certain literal-mindedness about the spiritualists that was bound to strike Steiner as simplistic. Most of them seem to feel that the 'riddle of existence' is solved by the assumption that we simply go on living in the 'next world'. On the other hand, there can be no doubt that the phenomenon of 'mediumship' really exists, and that there is strong evidence that mediums *have* been in touch with the dead. How could Steiner take up such an apparently negative attitude?

The answer can be found in a lecture called 'The History of Spiritism' delivered in Berlin on 30 May 1904. Here, he explains that there was a time in the past when man found it far more easy to contact the dead. 'The questions which the Spiritist wishes to answer today were during ancient times the concern of the so-called Mysteries.'

It was clearly understood that in each human being, spiritual forces slumber which in the average man are not developed. But spiritual forces slumber in human nature which can be awakened and developed by prolonged exercises, through stages of evolution that are described by the adherents of the Mysteries as very difficult. When a man had developed such forces in himself and had become able to make research into truth, the opinion was then held that such a researcher was related to the ordinary man just as one who can see is related to a man born blind. That is what those in the holy Mysteries aimed at.

According to Steiner, there were in the Middle Ages certain secret societies which led their members 'to the development of higher intuitive forces along the same lines that had been followed by the ancient Mysteries'. Then, with the rise of materialism, this direct, intuitive 'knowledge of higher worlds' slowly faded away.

And at this point, along came Spiritualism, with its mediums going into trances, its speaking trumpets flying around the room, its 'spirits' made of ectoplasm, and all the rest of the paraphernalia. The trouble with Spiritualism, according to Steiner, is that it encourages man to remain *blind*, instead of trying to achieve that direct, intuitive insight into the spirit world.

Oddly enough, Steiner thoroughly approved of Allan Kardec, the Frenchman who, in the mid-1850s, compiled an important body of 'spirit teachings' from automatic writing— *The Spirits' Book*. Kardec, like Steiner, accepted the reality of reincarnation. The rest of the French spiritualist movement, like the English spiritualists, flatly rejected it.

During these early years as a Theosophist, Steiner's main concern seems to have been to emphasize the continuity of the great religious tradition, from the mystery centres of primitive man to the creation of Anthroposophy. This had been one of the major themes of Madame Blavatsky; but Steiner took it further—a task for which he was well qualified through his knowledge of history and philosophy. Reading Wachsmuth's *Life*, it becomes very clear that Steiner believed that he could, single-handed, create a great religious movement comparable to Christianity or Islam. The time seemed propitious; there was a widespread hunger for 'spiritual values', and he had made many powerful allies: in 1904, for example, he stayed in Lugano as a guest of the industrialist Guenther Wagner, and began his 'conquest' of Switzerland. A student named Ludwig Kleeberg started a Theosophical group at the University of Munich, with the blessing of the Rector; in the following year, the movement spread to the University of Marburg. With his lectures, Steiner made an immediate impact that has led one German commentator* to compare him to Hitler. Kleeberg said of him:

> He began to lecture. His gaze, first turned outward, seemed now and then to be turned inward. He spoke out of an inner vision. The sentences were formed while he spoke. There was

Hitler, Steiner, Schreber, by Dr Wolfgang Treher.

power in his words. In his words dwelt the power to awaken
to life the slumbering unison of hearts. The hearts sensed
something of the power of which his words were formed, and
felt a strengthening of that tie which ... connected them with
the reality of a larger, broader and richer world.

This undoubtedly explains Steiner's enormous influence:
his ability to convey the feeling of a 'broader and richer
world'. Another disciple, the writer Albert Steffen, described
how he travelled to the ancient town of Augsburg to hear
Steiner lecture: 'as I walked through Augsburg's old streets, it
seemed to me as if everybody harboured this festival feeling,
as if it were poured into everyday life ... A fragrant breeze
arose, filling me with the bliss of knowledge as I inhaled the
sky's purple.' And as he came out of one of Steiner's lectures:
'It seemed to me that I felt spheres of consciousness which ...
we usually do not see, or at least, do not heed ...'. Steiner filled
his disciples with a sense of poetry, a feeling that the world
was about to be 'shattered, and rebuilt nearer to the heart's
desire'. So in a sense, it is not inappropriate to compare him to
Hitler who, in the mid-1930s, filled his audiences with the
feeling that the world was about to be transformed by a kind
of Wagnerian idealism, and raised to a new mythological
level of reality. Steiner's movement lacked the sinister under-
tones of Nazism, but its appeal was otherwise similar in many
ways. This helps to explain the increasingly bitter opposition he
experienced as the years went by; it was based upon the
feeling that anybody who can acquire such an enormous
following by preaching a fundamentally irrational doctrine
must be a charlatan and a trickster.

But during the early years, things went deceptively smoothly.
Steiner travelled and lectured, and took every opportunity to
visit historic sites and ancient monuments, always receiving
strong 'spiritual impressions'. In 1903 he was in London
again for another Theosophical congress, and launched his
magazine *Lucifer*. In 1904 he was at the Theosophical congress
in Amsterdam, and lectured throughout Germany. In 1905 he
lectured extensively on Richard Wagner, an artist for whom
he felt profound sympathy, since Wagner had laboured to
create his own 'Mystery centre' in Bayreuth, and had sub-

sequently crowned his career with a celebration of the Christian mystery in *Parsifal*. In 1906, Steiner enjoyed a remarkable personal triumph at the Theosophical congress in Paris, where he set up a kind of rival congress in the suburb of Passy, filling the house with distinguished Russians—like the mystical novelist Merejkovsky—and creating an atmosphere of enthusiasm and dedication. He finally met Edouard Schuré, author of *The Great Initiates*, whose drama *The Children of Lucifer* had been translated by Marie von Sivers; Schuré stated in print that at last he had met a genuine Initiate. He said of Steiner: 'The first impression was one of plastic power. When he spoke of the events and phenomena of the supersensible world, he spoke as one who was at home there . . . He did not describe; he beheld objects and scenes and made them visible, so that cosmic phenomena seemed to us like actual objects of the physical plane. When one listened to him, it was impossible to doubt his spiritual vision, which was as keen as physical sight . . .'.

In 1907, Steiner lectured in Germany, Czechoslovakia, and Switzerland, and was host to the Theosophical congress in Munich. It was his opportunity to show what he could do. The great concert hall was elaborately decorated in a way that would 'correspond in form and colour with the mood prevailing in the oral programme'. He encouraged the designers to give 'free expression to artistic feeling'—an approach which may be said to be the essence of Steiner's theory of art, drama, and education. He also broke with Theosophical tradition by presenting a Mystery drama. It was Schuré's *Sacred Drama of Eleusis*, an attempt to reconstruct the ancient Greek mystery drama. This is, in fact, a powerful piece of work that can bear comparison with Sophocles or Euripides: the story of how Persephone was dragged down to the underworld by Pluto—with the connivance of Zeus—and how she was rescued by Prince Triptolemos, son of the king of Eleusis. But the essence of the drama is the part played by the god Dionysus, Persephone's brother. Dionysus had been born when Zeus embraced Demeter, the earth goddess, in the form of a flaming astral serpent. But when the beautiful child was contemplating his own reflection in a mirror, the Titans threw themselves on him and tore him to pieces. Zeus destroyed them, and mankind was born from the vapours of their burning bodies, mingled with the vapours of the dismembered Dionysus. Demeter then seduced the lord of the gods against his will and conceived Persephone.

When Persephone is rescued from hell by the hero Triptolemos, Dionysus is suddenly reborn, for he is the spirit of heroism in human beings, which also creates men of genius. The reborn Dionysus takes Persephone, goddess of fertility, to be his bride, symbolizing the union of male genius and heroism with female fertility.

Whether Schuré's reconstruction of the Orphic Mystery drama bears any resemblance to the original is an open question. But it obviously appealed to Steiner because of its message that Dionysus—the primal ecstasy that springs from the heart of creation (Steiner knew his Nietzsche)—is reborn out of human heroism and genius, and unites with the female principle to save the world. (It may be significant that Marie von Sivers played Persephone.) Annie Besant, a stately, silver-haired lady, was evidently greatly impressed, and made amiable remarks about 'the land of great philosophers, poets and mystics'. For the German Theosophists, it was a moment of triumph to see their own leader standing as an equal beside the leader of the Theosophical Society, Madame Blavatsky's elected heir. Yet it was also the beginning of the split between Steiner and the Theosophists; it was at this congress that Annie Besant agreed that there should be a complete break between her own 'esoteric group' and Steiner's. It must have been obvious to her that what Steiner meant by esotericism had very little in common with the teachings of *The Secret Doctrine*.

Later that May, Steiner gave a lecture in Munich on 'The Theosophy of the Rosicrucians'. It could be regarded as an explicit gesture of rejection of Madame Blavatsky's esotericism, for according to Steiner, the Rosicrucian epoch of human development—which began in 1413—was a period in which initiation ceased to be restricted to a few adepts, and would become available to men engaged in the everyday business of the world. For those who entertain doubts about Steiner's visions of Atlantis and Lemuria, his notions about Rosicrucianism are bound to increase their scepticism. Rosicrucianism actually made its appearance on the historical scene in 1614, with the publication in Kassel, in Germany, of a pamphlet called *The Fame of the Fraternity of the Rosy Cross*. This declared that a certain Christian Rosenkreuz had spent life wandering around the East in search of occult wisdom; having found it, he formed a Brotherhood of the Rosy Cross to preserve it; buried in an unknown tomb, surrounded by lighted candles, his body remained undiscovered for a hundred and twenty years. Then disciples opened the tomb, which was lighted by 'another sun' in the middle of the ceiling—an interesting anticipation of electric light—and found the body 'whole and unconsumed'.

Rosenkreuz had been born in 1378, and had died, at the age of 106, in 1484; an inscription on the door of the tomb read 'I will open after 120 years'. It was opened in 1604, as prophesied.

The opening of the vault, according to the pamphlet, would to be drawn of a general reformation presaging the appearance of a 'divine light in the sky' (presumably the Second Coming).

A second pamphlet, the *Confessio*, followed a year later, hinting at marvellous occult knowledge. According to the *Fama*, 'interested parties' only had to make their interest known, and they would be contacted. Many people hastened to proclaim their interest in pamphlets; but, as far as is known, no one was ever contacted. Then in 1616, a third Rosicrucian work was published, *The Chemical Wedding of Christian Rosenkreuz*, a kind of allegorical novel, full of alchemical symbolism. It has since been established that the author of this work was a Tübingen clergyman named Johann Valentin Andreae, who later admitted that he had composed it as a 'ludibrium'—a joke. He denied being the author of the two earlier pamphlets, no doubt to avoid the indignation of would-be Initiates.

One expert on the Rosicrucians, Christopher McIntosh,* has suggested that the pamphlets were the brainchild of an idealistic group of young men who dreamed of 'a Europe free of religious dissension and basking in the light of the true Christian faith combined with science and learning'—a good

The Rosy Cross Unveiled (Aquarian Press, 1980).

summary of Steiner's own aims. Andreae wrote the *Chemical Wedding* in 1605, at the age of nineteen, and McIntosh speculates that the young idealists decided to resurrect its narrator, Christian Rosenkreuz, and make him the founder of a Brotherhood that might become a rallying point for the new religious revival. They were probably startled and shocked by the success of their hoax. Andreae himself published in 1619 a 'Utopian' work called *Christianopolis*. Rosicrucianism spread across Europe, rather like Freemasonry, and King Frederick-William of Prussia was initiated into the order in 1781. In England in the last quarter of the nineteenth century, a Rosicrucian Society became the Hermetic Order of the Golden Dawn, of which the poet W. B. Yeats was a member. In an essay on Christian Rosencrux (as he spelt it) Yeats wrote: 'I cannot get it out of my mind that this age of criticism is about to pass, and an age of imagination, of emotion, of moods, of revelation, about to come in its place; for certainly belief in a supersensual world is at hand.' Yeats is expressing the tremendous emotional hunger that helps to explain the immense success of Steiner's brand of Theosophy in the first decade of the twentieth century.

As an ironical footnote to Steiner's Rosicrucian revelations, we may note that one of his followers, Max Heindel, moved to America and wrote a book called *The Rosicrucian Cosmo-Conception or Mystic Christianity*, largely borrowed from Steiner; it became the basis of the American Rosicrucian Society, one of the most successful organizations of its kind. Even the crumbs from Steiner's table could feed multitudes.

Throughout 1908 Steiner continued to travel and lecture throughout Europe, and at an Annual General Meeting in October, Marie von Sivers was able to announce that, since the spring, the number of Steiner groups had increased from twenty-eight to thirty-seven. When Steiner stood up to speak, he began by announcing that it was his painful duty to expel a certain Dr Vollrath from the Society; it seemed that Dr Vollrath had formed a Literary Section without consulting Steiner, and had been guilty of various other acts of independence. Steiner followed up this excommunication with a lecture on the meaning of self-denial, renunciation, and sacrifice. After the meeting, a reception was given by Frau

Eliza von Moltke, wife of the chief of the army General Staff. General von Moltke was quoted as saying that all great philosophies had a gap—except Rudolf Steiner's Theosophy.

The chief event of the following year, 1909, was the publication of Steiner's book *Occult Science—an Outline*, regarded by many as his most important work. It repeats many of the things said in *Theosophy* and *Knowledge of Higher Worlds;* but its central section, a long chapter entitled 'The Evolution of the World and Man', goes a great deal further than the earlier books in describing man's evolution on Old Saturn, Old Sun, Old Moon, and so on. It should be born in mind that his earlier work on this topic—*Cosmic Memory*—had been published piecemeal in his magazine, and so had only been read by the faithful. This open publication, in a form available to the general public, may therefore be regarded as a gesture of supreme self-confidence. But a short postscript reveals that he is not wholly unconcerned about his critics. He offers an excellent summary of the kind of things they might say, accusing him of 'inconceivable ignorance of the rudiments of science'. Does that mean, asks Steiner, that he himself would dismiss the critic as an ignoramus? By no means, for he can quite understand how such a critic feels. All the same, he must inform him that he, Dr Steiner, has studied physics and chemistry, the philosophy of Kant, and has written books on Goethe, not to mention a defence of Haeckel. So let no one mistake him for a member of the lunatic fringe. He ends by remarking that 'anyone acquainted with supersensual research' will recognize that he has tried to communicate only 'what is permitted', although it is possible that, in the future, he may be allowed to say more.

In other words, Steiner was telling his critics that if they didn't like what he had to say, they knew what they could go and do . . . Such an attitude was bound to exasperate even the open-minded, an attitude that is betrayed by Maurice Maeterlinck in the final paragraph of his remarks on Steiner in *The Great Secret*: 'When all is taken into account, we realize once more, as we lay his works aside, what we realized after reading most of the other mystics: that what he calls "the great drama of [occult] knowledge" . . . should rather be called the great drama of essential and invincible ignorance.' If a man as tolerant and undogmatic as Maeterlinck could become so irritable, it is hardly surprising that less broad-minded critics should feel that Steiner was a kind of pestilence that ought to be stamped out. As Steiner's hold over the faithful continued to increase, so did the resentment of people who felt that the Steinerites were a crowd of besotted lunatics enslaved by a confidence trickster. And this, it must be admitted, was to some extent his own fault. His fellow 'occultist' Gurdjieff, who had just embarked on his own career as a teacher in Russia, took care that his own esoteric teaching should remain secret, and so never incurred the resentment that eventually inflicted such blows on the Anthroposophical movement. Steiner could easily have done the same thing: used his books to spread the idea of 'spiritual development', and reserved the 'cosmological' teachings for the faithful. In retrospect, it seems that his failure to do so was his greatest single mistake.

For Steiner, 1909 was a crucial year in the history of the German Theosophical movement, being the beginning of a new seven-year cycle. Steiner attached great importance to seven-year cycles—in the history of movements as well as of individuals. He was later to declare that the year 1909 was the beginning of 'a very special time', in which those who wished to be close to Christ could achieve it in 'a quite different way from that of previous times'. This was because there was a 'new action of Christ in the etheric world'. This may also explain why, during 1909, he became increasingly outspoken against the 'orientalizing' tendencies of the Theosophical Society.

The year 1910 was as hectic as previous years, beginning with lectures in Scandinavia, then in Berlin, then in Cologne, Stuttgart, and Munich, then in Vienna; after this he travelled through Italy to Sicily, and lectured in Rome on 'The Intervention of Great Personalities who share in our Earth Evolution'. There he met a British painter named Harry Collison, who became an Anthroposophist and went off to found Societies in America, Australia, and New Zealand.

On his return from the Italian tour, Steiner spent a few weeks dashing off a play called *The Portal of Initiation*, a 'Mystery drama' which was presented in August at the

Munich congress, preceded by Schuré's *Drama of Eleusis*.
Steiner designed the set and costumes, dictating the colours
in accordance with Goethe's colour theory. All the actors
were amateurs, trained by Marie von Sivers. The play was
performed before an audience of two thousand people.
Drama critics were not invited.

It is difficult to speak with detachment about the four
Mystery dramas (for Steiner was to write another one in each
of the three succeeding years). For Wachsmuth they are 'the
blest fruit of the interplay of spiritual vision and artistic
formative power'. Stewart Easton emphasizes their kinship
with the older Greek tragedies, particularly those of Aeschylus,
except in the length of the speeches. The non-Anthroposophist
is bound to find them over-long, incredibly tedious, and at
times painfully naive. People stand around and argue at
enormous length about 'dry, prosaic reason' and the need for
spiritual vision, and utter comments like: 'With your last
words I am in full agreement', or 'The weight of this objection
I can feel.' A scene may begin with words like:

'Good morning, Sophia. I hope I am not disturbing you?'

'Not at all, Estella, you are very welcome.'

Or:

'Dear mother, I would so much like to hear the story from you, of
which Cilli so often spoke, some time ago . . .'.

Schuré's Mystery drama has power, economy, and action;
Steiner's plays ramble on gently, like a Steiner lecture
converted into a Wagner libretto—but, unfortunately, without
the music. No doubt Wachsmuth and Easton are right when
they insist that they should be judged by their content, not by
their literary quality. But the need to make such allowances
underlines one of the basic problems of esoteric movements:
that the very nature of their belief tends to irritate and repel
non-believers because it seems to involve a deliberate suspen-
sion of their critical faculties. It would be pleasant to be able to
say: 'I cannot accept most of Steiner's ideas, but his Mystery
plays are nevertheless an exciting and moving experience.'

In fact, the Mystery dramas constitute a gulf between believers and non-believers instead of a bridge. Whatever their underlying content, they are 'serious' in quite the wrong way. The major character is a spiritual teacher named Benedictus, obviously Steiner himself. Most of the other characters are his disciples. Ahriman, Lucifer and various spirits also appear— the tone is often reminiscent of *Faust*, but a *Faust* without poetry and without the concentration. For the non-believer the whole atmosphere has a flavour of Sunday school. It is not Steiner's sincerity that is in question here, but his judgement.

This view receives a certain support from a book on Steiner by a man who was to become one of his most important followers, Friedrich Rittelmeyer, a Protestant theologian. At the time he came upon Steiner's work—in 1910—Rittelmeyer was one of the most popular and influential preachers in Berlin. When asked to lecture on 'religious striving in the present time', he decided to make the acquaintance of Theosophy. Annie Besant's variety sickened him: 'The spirit, as presented by them, was a mixture of ancient tradition and subjective emotionalism.' He found Steiner altogether more interesting, but was thoroughly put off by *Occult Science*. 'It upset me, for I simply could not wade through it. If I read for any length of time, a feeling of nausea came over me.' Finally, in 1911, he attended a Steiner lecture, and was not impressed by the audience. 'A certain passive, sensation-mongering mentality troubled me.' Neither did Steiner impress him as a speaker; he found his style 'round-about and involved'. He was grimly amused by the crowds of admiring disciples who thronged around Steiner after the lecture. It was not until he heard Steiner lecture on Goethe that he began to feel that 'this was a kingly mind in the realms of knowledge'. Even so, he found the next lecture he attended a disappointment, and was irritated by Steiner's fur coat and flowing black tie. But Rittelmeyer, like Steiner, was obsessed by the figure of Christ, and it was Steiner's 'Christology' that eventually formed the link between them; Steiner was later to entrust to Rittelmeyer the organization of an Anthroposophical Christian Community.

The presentation—and design—of the Mystery dramas led Steiner to give new consideration to the problem of art in general and dramatic art in particular. Wagner had united music and drama. The Russian composer Alexander Scriabin was attempting something even more ambitious, a new art form that would involve music, drama, dance, and even colours blending on a screen—produced by a machine of his own invention called a 'colour organ'. His music had a swooning, ecstatic quality, and seemed to be an illustration of his belief that some great apocalypse was at hand when spirit would finally overcome matter, and man would become a god. When he died, of blood poisoning, in 1915, he was working on his greatest project, a Mystery that would take place in a temple and involve hundreds of virgins dressed in white robes. In 1911, he was regarded as one of the most significant artistic figures of his time.

Another was the dancer Isadora Duncan; she also believed that feelings could be danced, and swayed gracefully around the stage with bare feet and wearing a Grecian tunic. A rather more systematic version of the same thing was the method developed by the Swiss composer Emile Jaques-Dalcroze, who taught his pupils music by training them in harmonious bodily movement; from merely performing gymnastics, his pupils would gradually learn to improvise body movements to express a whole symphony or concerto.

Steiner called his own version of the dance 'Eurythmy', insisting at the same time that it should not be confused with the art of dancing. Its aim was to 'cause a person or group of persons to carry out movements which bring to expression the element of music and language in visible form, just as the organs of language and song do it in audible form. The whole human being or group of human beings becomes a larynx ...' Steiner was striving for the same kind of unity that Scriabin had dreamed of achieving in his own Mystery. And this, in turn, would be an integral part of a still greater unity of art, science, and religion—thus reuniting the three components that should never have become separated. Eurythmy was developed by a seventeen-year-old girl, Lory Smits—in close association with Steiner—in 1912 (although Steiner was toying with the idea as early as 1908), and was first presented in public at the Munich festival in the following years.

We can catch an interesting glimpse of the impression Steiner made on people during this period in the diaries of the young Franz Kafka, a writer who would acquire a worldwide reputation only after his death in 1924, at the age of forty. In 1911, when Kafka was in his mid-twenties, Steiner delivered a number of lectures in Berlin, and Kafka went to hear him. The tone is ironic; obviously, Kafka is inclined to feel hostile.

Theosophical lectures by Dr Rudolf Steiner, Berlin. Rhetorical effect: Comfortable discussion of the objections of opponents, the listener is astonished at this strong opposition, further development and praise of these objections, the listener becomes worried, complete immersion in these objections as though they were nothing else, the listener now considers any refutation as completely impossible and is more than satisfied with a cursory description of the possibility of a defence.

Continual looking at the palm of the extended hand. Omission of the period. In general, the spoken sentence starts off from the speaker with its initial capital letter, curves in its course, as far as it can, out to the audience, and returns with the period to the speaker. But if the period is omitted then the sentence, no longer in check, falls upon the listener immediately with full force.

Two days later, Kafka's account of another lecture is even more ironically detached and hostile:

Dr Steiner is so very much taken up with his absent disciples. At the lecture the dead press so about him. Hunger for knowledge? But do they really need it? Apparently, though— Sleeps two hours. Ever since someone once cut off his electric light he has always had a candle with him—He stood very close to Christ—He produced his play in Munich (you can study it all the year there and won't understand it). He designed the costumes, composed the music—He instructed a Chemist . . .

He is, perhaps, not the greatest contemporary psychic scholar, but he alone has been assigned the task of uniting theosophy and science. And that is why he knows everything too. Once a botanist came to his native village, a great master of the occult. He enlightened him.

That I would look up Dr Steiner was interpreted to me by the lady as the beginning of recollection. The lady's doctor, when the first signs of influenza appeared in her, asked Dr Steiner for a remedy, prescribed this for the lady, and restored her to health with it immediately. A French woman said goodbye to him with '*au revoir*'. Behind her back he shook his head. In two months she died. A similar case in Munich. A Munich doctor cures people with colours decided upon by Dr Steiner. He also sends invalids to the picture gallery with instructions to concentrate for half an hour or longer on a certain painting.

End of the Atlantic world, lemuroid destruction, and now through egoism. We live in a period of decision. The efforts of Dr Steiner will succeed only if the Ahrimanian forces do not get the upper hand.

He eats two litres of emulsion of almonds and fruits that grow in the air.

He communicates with his absent disciples by means of thought-forms which he transmits to them without bothering about them after they are generated. But they soon wear out and he must replace them.

Mrs F.: 'I have a poor memory.' Dr St.: 'Eat no eggs.'

Clearly, Kafka regarded Steiner as a fake messiah. This probably tells us more about Kafka than about Steiner. Yet it also enables us to understand why so many people regarded Steiner with hostility. Kafka's own attitude towards him was obviously ambivalent. Shortly after this last lecture, he decided to pay a visit to Steiner, which he describes in detail. Kafka quotes his 'prepared address' to Steiner—how he felt that a great part of his being was moving towards theosophy, but at the same time that he had the greatest fear of it: 'That is to say, I am afraid it will result in a new confusion which would be very bad for me, because even my present unhappiness consists only of confusion.' He goes on to describe his confusion and unhappiness at great length, and then explains that in certain moments when he is writing, he experiences the state that Steiner seems to describe as clairvoyance. He is tempted to give up his job to become a writer, and yet realizes that this is a thoroughly impractical idea. What advice can Steiner give him?

He listened very attentively without apparently looking at me at all, entirely devoted to my words. He nodded from time to time, which he seems to consider an aid to strict concentration. At first a quiet head cold disturbed him, his nose ran, he kept working his handkerchief deep into his nose, one finger at each nostril.

And that is all Kafka has to tell us about Rudolf Steiner. He sees with the thoroughly unsympathetic eye of a young man of talent who rather resents the fame of other people. Yet if we try to place ourselves behind Steiner's eyes, looking at this nervous, pale young man who talks rapidly and at inordinate length, admitting that he is thoroughly confused, and pouring out his psychological problems, it is impossible not to feel that Steiner deserves admiration for his almost saintly forbearance. Of the crowds of people who demanded personal interviews, probably only one in a thousand happened to possess genius, as Kafka did. But this was hardly any consolation for Steiner. The endless queue of time-wasters undermined his health and finally destroyed him.

During this period, relations with the London-based Theosophical Society were becoming increasingly strained. This was due largely to Steiner's repudiation of 'orientalism', and his increasing emphasis on the importance of Christ: in 1911, he had even gone so far as to say: 'To grasp the idea of freedom without the idea of salvation by Christ ought not to be found possible by mankind; on that condition alone is the idea of freedom justified'—a somewhat baffling statement for the author of *The Philosophy of Freedom*.

What made the rupture between the English and the German Society inevitable was the discovery of a new 'messiah' by the English Theosophist The Revd Charles Leadbeater. In 1909, Leadbeater was on a beach near Adyar, India, when he saw an exceptionally beautiful Indian child. Leadbeater claimed that he was instantly impressed by the boy's remarkable aura, but the fact that Leadbeater was a pederast may also have played its part. Leadbeater persuaded the boy's father, a minor civil servant who held a post in the Theosophical Society in Madras, to allow him to take Jiddu, and his younger brother Nitya, into his house. Mrs Besant met Jiddu and was convinced that he was the latest incarnation of the master Maitreya, and that he would be the saviour of the twentieth century. Leadbeater, who—like Steiner—claimed to be able to divine past incarnations, even wrote an account of the boy's previous thirty lives, starting in 22,662 BC.

The German Theosophists were naturally outraged by this attempt to foist a new messiah on them, not only because it was in direct contradiction to Steiner's teachings about Christ, but because it looked suspiciously like an attempt to upstage their own German Messiah. Steiner was offered a 'package deal'; if he would accept Krishnamurti as the new Christ, he could be John the Baptist; apparently he rejected this with indignation. When, in 1911, The Society founded the Order of the Star of the East, with Krishnamurti as its object of adoration, the break became inevitable. Steiner declared that no one who joined the new Order could remain a member of *his* Society. Mrs Besant retaliated by having the charter of the German Society revoked by the General Council. (Fourteen German lodges remained loyal; the rest went with Steiner.) The German Society sent her a telegram demanding her resignation. And finally, in February 1913, Steiner changed the name of the German branch to the Anthroposophical Society. The Theosophists, understandably—and, on the whole, justly—accused him of using the Society purely as a means of forwarding his own ambitions; certainly, Steiner would never have achieved his large following if he had remained an independent lecturer.

Apart from the founding of the Anthroposophical Society, 1913 was much like the previous years. Steiner undertook nine foreign lecture tours, wrote a new Mystery drama, *The Soul's Awakening*, supervised the first presentation of Eurythmy in public, and turned his attention increasingly to the problem of diet and nutrition, condemning the consumption of meat and alcohol. But he was not dogmatic about it, and did not insist that all Anthroposophists should be vegetarians. When one of them admitted to him he still dreamed about ham, Steiner replied: 'Better eat ham than think ham.' And although he disapproved of smoking (he had given it up himself, and switched to snuff) he made no attempt to force his views on his secretary Wachsmuth.

Now the Anthroposophical Society had become a separate entity, and showed every sign of continuing to expand, it was necessary to give some thought to the question of its headquarters. To begin with, Steiner wanted a theatre suitable for presenting his Mystery dramas—he was now planning a fifth. The obvious choice was Munich, Germany's artistic capital, but Stuttgart, which had a large Steiner Society, was a strong rival. Then, to everyone's surprise, the Munich authorities turned down the plan to build an Anthroposophical Society headquarters and theatre; they had no desire to see their city turned into the Bayreuth of a peculiar religious sect. Fortunately, an alternative had already presented itself. A Swiss Anthroposophist, Dr. Emil Grossheintz, had purchased a hill at Dornach in Switzerland, and he wished it to be used for some purpose connected with Anthroposophy; Steiner had already been to inspect it when the Munich authorities turned down his application. Steiner decided immediately that he would build his theatre at Dornach, and lost no time in designing it. Predictably—in view of his ideas on plasticity and Nature—it was a place with few right angles and straight lines. The idea was to create a building, a temple, that looked as if it might have grown like a tree. The building was called the Goetheanum, a name more-or-less unpronounceable for English readers. The foundation stone was laid on 20 September 1913, large sums of money having been collected or pledged at the Munich festival of the previous month.

As Steiner made a speech and laid the foundation stone—composed of a double pentagonal dodecahedron—a tremendous storm broke, virtually drowning his voice. As night fell prematurely, the small band of followers lighted torches, while Steiner spoke of the increasing forces of Ahriman, 'who intends to spread darkness and chaos'. It was as if the elements were trying to tell him that it was the worst possible moment to build a temple.

Steiner was hoping to complete the building by August 1914, so it could be used to present his fifth Mystery drama (which, in the event, remained unwritten). But by the new year it was obvious that the funds they had collected were about to run out; Steiner quickly organized a series of lectures to the faithful, emphasizing the importance of this joint project for the future salvation of humanity. More money flowed in; many Anthroposophists gave up their jobs and moved to Dornach to help build the Goetheanum. By April 1914, the framework was in place, and the two great domes were ready to be covered with slate. Most of the Goetheanum was built of wood, in accordance with Steiner's feeling that it should be 'natural'. This was a decision that everyone would have reason to regret.

When the Archduke Franz Ferdinand was assassinated at Sarajevo on 28 June 1914, it became increasingly clear that the August festival would not take place. Steiner was on his way to Bayreuth in early August when the war broke out. Steiner was forced to rush back to Dornach, surrounded by increasing chaos: guards on every bridge, soldiers marching, railway stations jammed with people. With the aid of an Anthroposophist who was also a railway official, Steiner and Marie von Sivers were hastily pushed into a compartment of a train in Stuttgart; hours later, they were back across the Swiss border. Marie von Sivers remarks: 'During this terrible grey night, the world had changed, and the expression of a nightmare which rested during those days upon Dr Steiner's face, his pain on account of humanity, was almost unbearable.'

For all his optimism and determination to continue, Steiner must have sensed that this was the end of his dream. He had hoped that the building of the Goetheanum signalled a new epoch in the evolution of mankind, the beginning of a religion that would sweep across the world as irresistibly as Christianity in the first century or Muhammadism in the seventh. Now it was very clear that the world had other things on its mind beside religion. As far as Europe was concerned, Anthroposophy belonged to the past, not the future.

Eight

Disaster

ALTHOUGH for Europe the war was an unmitigated disaster, for Steiner it had its compensations. He was able to work quietly at the task of completing the Goetheanum, with the aid of many disciples, to spend time in reflection, and to write some of his most significant books, like *Riddles of Man* and *Riddles of the Soul*. He was still able to travel and lecture to a remarkable extent—for, as Wachsmuth remarks, the time of endless difficulties with travel permits had not yet arrived—but it was no longer at the same frantic pace as in the pre-war years. He was patriotic, but in a non-nationalistic sense; he lectured in many German cities on the mission of the German spirit, which he saw as acting as a balance between the opposing forces of Russia on the one hand and Britain and the United States on the other. At Dornach, many nationalities, including those at war with one another, continued to gather and work in harmony. It was now apparent that the difficulties about building in Munich had been a blessing in disguise.

The war was going badly with Germany, and, oddly enough, many blamed Steiner. For a long time Germany had been looking for an excuse to go to war against Russia, believing that Russian industrial development constituted a long-term menace to Germany. But when this chance came, with the Serbian problem, the Kaiser suddenly became jittery, and it was his wife who was sent in by his generals to tell him to 'be a man' and declare war. The generals were convinced that Germany could not lose. The plan devised by General von Schlieffen involved hurling all the German forces against the French and smashing them in one tremendous blow, then turning the army against the Russians. Von Moltke—husband of Steiner's disciple—was Commander-in-Chief. But the

Kaiser's jitters had infected Moltke; he could not make up his mind whether to take the Schlieffen gamble, or play safe and divide his forces. He asked Steiner to go to see him, but it was impossible to arrange a meeting immediately. By the time Steiner arrived at Coblenz on 27 August 1914, the major decisions had been taken, and the German offensive was already in trouble. As a result of that initial mistake of von Moltke's, the war turned into a slogging match fought between two entrenched armies, and the seed of Germany's defeat was planted. Whether Steiner could have given Moltke the advice he needed if they had met three weeks earlier is a matter for speculation. At all events, Moltke made his fatal decisions, was relieved of his command, and died two years later. When it was known that Steiner had been to see him at a crucial moment, he was widely blamed for interfering where he had no business. The misunderstandings that had so far been confined to his doctrines were now directed at his person, and took on a new dimension of malice.

Steiner himself evidently felt that the war marked some kind of turning point in the history of his movement, for he abandoned the idea of the fifth Mystery play, and instead concentrated on producing the first complete stage version of *Faust*, including the second part. In December 1915, he drilled his amateur actors to speak Austrian dialect in traditional Christmas plays, and revealed that, under different circumstances, he would have made a successful commercial director.

According to Steiner's theory of seven-year cycles, 1916 marked a new beginning. He had devoted the last seven years to blending art and Anthroposophy; now, in a world divided by war, he felt it was time to turn his thoughts to social questions, and to the reconstruction of civilization after the war. In a book called *Riddles of the Soul* (*Von Seelenrätsel*) he spoke at length of his teacher Brentano, and in one long footnote, threw off an idea that came to be regarded as one of his major pronouncements: that man's main faculties—thinking, feeling, willing—are carried out through different parts of his physical organism. Thinking involves the head and nervous system, feeling involves the breathing rhythms and circulation of the blood, willing involves the metabolic system—such as digestion. Thinking is conscious, feeling is semi-conscious—like breathing, which is 'automatic', but can still be influenced by the will—while willing belongs wholly to the realm of the unconscious, like the growing of the nails or hair.

When Steiner turned his thought to social reconstruction, he found himself thinking naturally in this 'threefold' terminology. Like the traditional division of man into body and soul, the division of society into Church and State must be an over-simplification. According to Steiner, society should consist of the equivalent of head, circulatory system, and metabolic system. The head should be human creativity, the circulatory system should be the political government, while the metabolic system should be the economic system. These three he linked with the French revolutionary ideal of Liberty, Equality, and Fraternity. The essence of creativity is liberty: creators cannot be equals, or even brothers; they must stand alone. The business of government should be to make sure that, as political animals, men are equals. This concept of equality cannot—obviously—apply to the business community; *its* purpose should be to aim at fraternity, at producing wealth and goods for the good of the community, not the individual. The result should be a threefold social order—or common-wealth—in which each part preserves its separate identity, yet works harmoniously with the other two.

Early in 1917, as it became clear that Russia was drifting towards social revolution, a distinguished Anthroposophist, Count Otto Lerchenfeld, a member of the Bavarian state council, asked Steiner for his views on social reconstruction after the war. The two sat together for three days and discussed the idea of the 'threefold commonwealth', and when Lerchenfeld finally left, he was bubbling with enthusiasm. With the aid of another Anthroposophist, Count Ludwig Polzer-Hoditz, a memorandum was drawn up. The intention was to send it to all the statesmen of Europe, including the Allies. Polzer-Hoditz passed on the memorandum to his brother, who was the chief councillor of the new emperor, Karl of Austria. Whether Karl read it or not is unknown; at all events, Steiner heard no more of it.

This is hardly surprising. What Steiner was offering was, in fact, a form of anarchism. The state is to have its authority reduced; its main business is simply to ensure that all citizens have equal rights. It has no role to play in the economy—that is the task of the 'economic domain'—and none in education, which is the task of the cultural domain. Moreover, the aim of the business domain is not to make excessive profits, but simply to supply the goods that everyone needs. The cultural leaders will fertilize economic life with new ideas, and will in turn have their own basic needs taken care of.

The idea is inspiring, but the objections are obvious. Throughout history, politicians have been in charge of central government, and have never shown the slightest inclination to see their power reduced—hence those bitter struggles between Church and State in the Middle Ages. Politicians *become* politicians because they are interested in power. Neither have businessmen ever shown the slightest inclination to devote their talents to the general good and turn their backs on the motive of personal enrichment; businessmen become businessmen because they are interested in money. As to the 'guardians of culture' — thinkers, artists, teachers — they have never yet succeeded in exercising any real influence either on businessmen or politicians. Steiner's vision of a commonwealth in which the artists and thinkers are, quite literally, the head, while businessmen and politicians listen to them respectfully and agree to take a back seat, is charming and delightful to contemplate, but totally unrealistic. The fate of Steiner's own memorandum should have taught him what practical politicians think of idealistic amateurs.

Steiner was undeterred by objections such as these; he dismissed them as the fruit of old-fashioned materialistic thinking. Neither did he regard it as any objection that he had no practical plan through which his ideas could be implemented. He was convinced that the 'threefold commonwealth' would come about of itself once it was understood by men of good will; in fact, he prophesied that it would inevitably come to pass during the next forty years. As far as he was concerned, the chief problem was simply to make sure that everyone heard about it. And the publication of his book *The Threefold Commonwealth* seemed to demonstrate that there was enormous appetite for Steiner's type of idealism; it became something of a bestseller, and was translated into many languages. As the war came to an end, Steiner once again launched himself into feverish activity, lecturing all over Europe, but concentrating most of his attention on Germany. And while a young ex-corporal named Adolf Hitler was inspiring the German Workers' Party by preaching nationalism and anti-semitism, Steiner was telling his own audiences to turn their minds to higher things: 'Instead of thinking about the very next requirements of the moment, a broader conception of life must now take place which will strive with strong thinking to comprehend the evolutionary forces of modern humanity . . .'.

Steiner was startled by the bitterness of the opposition he encountered. In the early years of the century, he had been able to tell the workers that Marxism was intellectually unsound without arousing too much resentment. But conditions were now changed; half Germany was starving; the mark was almost valueless. After the Russian revolution, the German communists felt that their moment had come, and they were intolerant of half-baked anarchists who felt Utopia was round the corner. They forbade their members to attend Steiner's meetings. As for the Nazis, they were quite determined to see the communists destroyed; Steiner was simply an irrelevance. But when he preached against patriotism, and announced that his 'threefold commonwealth' would gradually erode all national boundaries, they began to regard him as a menace. So his meetings were interrupted by hecklers. Things came to a climax in May 1922, when Steiner lectured in ten German cities in two weeks. In Munich—Hitler's city—young Nazis continually interrupted his talk on 'Anthroposophy and Spiritual Knowledge'. Then, in the Four Seasons Hotel, he was physically attacked, and only the prompt intervention of his friends saved him from injury; Steiner had to escape ignominiously by the back door. After that, his lecture agents decided that, for the time being at any rate, it was too dangerous to book him in Germany.

Steiner went on immediately to a West-East conference in Vienna, at which he was one of the major speakers. Wachsmuth notes: 'A large part of the press was either extremely reserved or hostile . . .'. Steiner was experiencing this reaction more and more frequently, and it worried him. Wachsmuth mentions his 'acute distress' when an 'aggressive pastor' published a pamphlet full of 'crass falsehoods'. Wachsmuth himself is obviously baffled that a man of Steiner's sincerity and benevolence should be so violently attacked, and puts it down to sheer human wickedness. He seems unaware that most people saw Steiner as a woolly-minded crank, full of preposterous ideas borrowed from Madame Blavatsky, and that there was a general feeling that it was time he met his come-uppance.

In August 1922, Steiner went to Oxford to speak at an educational conference. Since the end of the war, Steiner had acquired a new reputation as an eminent educationalist. An Anthroposophist named Emil Molt, who ran the Waldorf-Astoria tobacco factory in Stuttgart, asked Steiner's advice about setting up a school for the children of his workers. Here Steiner was in his element; he was an educationalist by nature and vocation. Above all, he understood that the task of the teacher is to persuade children that they *want* to be educated— a concept that would have struck most Germans as perversely paradoxical. The Waldorf school in Stuttgart was an immediate success; within a few years it had eleven hundred pupils, and hundreds of others had to be rejected. So when Steiner lectured at Oxford, he was able to stand as an equal among eminent educationalists, including Professor Gilbert Murray; when the *Manchester Guardian* said that 'the entire congress finds its central point in the personality and teaching of Dr Rudolf Steiner' it meant, of course, his educational theories, not his 'spiritual' teachings.

Back in Dornach in September, another important event took place: the founding of the 'Christian Community'. Steiner was presenting a course of lectures for theologians, and many of those present felt that a new religious impulse was needed. Steiner himself had come to recognize that Anthroposophy—the quest for 'spiritual knowledge'—cannot replace the daily practice of religion, with its rituals and sacraments. It was an important recognition that seemed to mark a change in attitude, for the Steiner of ten years earlier had seemed to feel that the new Orphic Mysteries could replace the element of ritual. Now he told the assembled ministers and theologians that if a religious revival was to be achieved, then the bearers of the message would have to be

'God-inspired'. It furnishes additional evidence of Steiner's charismatic personality that many of them decided to accept the challenge, and gave up their own pulpits to serve the new movement. The Christian Community was founded under the leadership of Friedrich Rittelmeyer; its forty-five priests included a Buddhist scholar and three women. Steiner provided a sacrament called The Act of Consecration of Man, which Rittelmeyer found deeply moving. There were some members of the Anthroposophical Society who thought that Steiner had now founded an Anthroposophical religion; on 30 December 1922, Steiner had to deliver a lecture that was, in effect, a mild rebuke. But when the news of the Christian Community percolated through to the outer world, it was inevitable that the same misunderstanding should arise, and Steiner suddenly found that he had a host of new enemies within the established Church.

The 'come-uppance' that his opponents had been hoping for arrived with disastrous suddenness on New Year's Eve 1922. That evening, Steiner delivered the last lecture of a course on the Spiritual Communion of Mankind. Wachsmuth says: 'In the great domed hall of the building people listened to his words. The mighty columns also, the forms of their capitals, the paintings of the dome in the lofty work of art of this most living of all human buildings spoke to them of spiritual action and the sense of sacrifice, of a decade of creative moulding through a human being who was leading towards the spiritual communion of mankind.' The deeply moved audience left at about ten o'clock. Soon after, a watchman noticed smoke in the White Hall. No fire could be found, until a wall in the south wing was broken into; it was burning inside. The fire brigade arrived quickly; Anthroposophists rushed into the building to rescue sculptures and paintings. But by morning, little was left of the Goetheanum but its concrete foundations. Most commentators suggest that the fire was due to arson, but the fact that it began inside a wall suggests an electrical fault.

Steiner bore the blow with dignity. He was heard to mutter: 'Much work and many years.' But the next day, he ascended the rostrum in the nearby joinery shop and announced that the play scheduled for that afternoon would still take place. And in the evening, Steiner gave a lecture on Science in World History in the workshop. In the disaster, he had shown himself to be a true leader.

The building of a new Goetheanum began immediately; Steiner once again designed it. The new building was made of concrete.

The destruction of the Goetheanum seems to have brought to a head Steiner's own inner sense of dissatisfaction; on 23 January 1923, he delivered an address to the Society that was a powerful rebuke. Anthroposophy, he said, was losing its sense of inner purpose. People had started 'premature undertakings' and failed to follow them through. What was needed was a new spirit of dedication. He began to brood on a new constitution for the Society, and on the reorganization of foreign branches. Then, with all the old nervous energy, he threw himself once more into lectures and international travel: Switzerland, Germany, Czechoslovakia, England and Wales, Austria, and Holland. Wachsmuth was greatly impressed when Steiner climbed with him to the plateau containing the stone circle of Penaenmawr, discoursing all the way on the Mysteries of the Druids and of Mithras, and was still apparently unfatigued when they came down again.

Steiner's discourse on this occasion is a remarkable example of his genuine insight into the past. In 1923 very little was known about prehistoric stone circles, and they were generally assumed to be of 'Druid' origin (the Druids being a Celtic priesthood who arrived in England from Europe around 600 BC). We now know that most stone circles predate the Druids by many centuries, some as much as two thousand years. Yet in spite of his mistaken assumption about the Druids, Steiner recognized that the circles were basically astronomical calculators, and that the stones were somehow aligned with surrounding peaks.

> He suggested that I look at the peaks of the mountain domes surrounding the plateau, and described to me . . . how the Druid priests, through viewing the signs of the zodiac passing along the horizon in the course of the year experienced the spiritual cosmos . . . He explained how they determined the consecration of the festivals and the cults of the year according to these cosmic rhythms, and gave their priestly directions to

those belonging to their communities; how the occurrences in the course of the year had to be spiritually mirrored in the cult, and physically even in the carrying out of agricultural labour. He spoke of the experience of sunlight and shadow in the stone chamber of the ancient sacred place, and of the spreading of the visions there received and their impulses into the expanses of the earthly environment . . .

More than half a century after Steiner's death, this sounds like sheer inspiration. In Steiner's day, monuments like Stonehenge were assumed to be the 'Druid' equivalent of churches; it is only in the past decade or so that unorthodox archaeologists like Professor Alexander Thom and Gerald Hawkins, and unorthodox astronomers like Fred Hoyle, have shown them to be astronomical calculators, and that an even more unorthodox fraternity known as 'ley hunters' have suggested theories of their purpose that are practically identical with Steiner's.

This provides an interesting clue to the riddle of Steiner's 'spiritual insight'. It was not sufficiently accurate to enable him to distinguish between a late Neolithic site and an Iron Age site, yet where the actual purpose of the site is concerned, it seems to go straight to the heart of the matter. This seems to confirm the suspicion that arose in connection with his visit to Tintagel: that Steiner possessed some deeply intuitive insight into such matters, but that when he attempted to bring it into logical—and historical— focus he was liable to go hopelessly awry.

Steiner's insight into the natural rhythms of the earth formed the basis of his agricultural theories, whose influence after his death was to be as widespread as that of his educational theories. Wachsmuth explains how in 1922 Steiner's followers asked him for some practical suggestions about agriculture, and were told that they must acquire 'preparations' out of the realm of plants and animals, and then expose these 'in a particular way to the rhythms of the cosmic and earthly forces in summer and winter so that the forces beneficial to life . . . might be concentrated and enriched.' They were told to take cow horns and fill them with various natural substances, then leave them buried in the earth for the winter. When they were dug up, the preparations were stirred vigorously into water, and the resulting mixture used as a fertilizer. Steiner was strongly opposed to chemical fertilizers and insecticides, and there can be no doubt that his 'biological farming' methods were based on his 'spiritual insights' into the farming methods of prehistoric man, as well as on Goethe's vision of nature.

Steiner's medical insights were equally revolutionary, and just as far ahead of their time. His starting point—inevitably—was his Goethean 'anti-reductionism'. The reductionist theory accepts that the cells of our bodies interact according to some more-or-less 'chemical' law which governs their reproduction and growth. The anti-reductionist view was expressed by Dr D. W. Smithers when he said that it was as impossible to deduce the form of a human being from the study of his cells as to deduce the rules of billiards from the study of individual billiard balls.* And at the turn of the century, the biologist Hans Driesch argued that living organisms can only be understood as *wholes*, and that if they have 'purpose' in their growth, then this purpose is something quite separate from their mechanical bits and pieces. In the 1930s, two Yale professors, Harold Burr and F. S. C. Northrop, connected delicate voltmeters to trees and discovered regular seasonal variations in their electric fields. Burr went on to conclude that living cells are held together and 'arranged' by these fields in the same way that iron filings are 'arranged' by a magnet. In fact, the life-field (or L-field) is a kind of jelly mould into which the living matter is poured. This is, of course, coming very close to Goethe's view that nature is controlled by spirit.

It would follow that, for example, a cancer—which consists of normally healthy cells running riot—is due to some kind of breakdown of control of the L-field, and that therefore, in a sense, a cancer is controllable by will (bearing in mind Steiner's insistence that will operates basically on the metabolic level).

A pupil of Steiner's named Ita Wegman asked about the application of his principles to medicine, and as a result went on to found the Arlesheim Clinic, based on principles that

*Quoted from *Work Arising from the Life of Rudolf Steiner*, edited by John Davy, p. 132.

would now be called 'holistic'. As with Steiner's educational theories, the movement has spread until it has become worldwide.

Steiner's theories on medicine included important insights into the mentally ill, and these were developed by Dr Friedrich Husemann, who founded the Wiesneck Sanatorium at Buchenbach. A request for advice about mentally ill children led to the founding of an Institute for Therapeutic Education at Jena. Steiner's belief in reincarnation played an important part in his attitude to handicapped children and to mongols; he taught that they had been placed in sick, misshapen bodies or burdened with underdeveloped brains for 'karmic' reasons, and that a certain development *is* possible with love and understanding. His attitude was based on his own personal experience with the mentally retarded Otto Specht, who was totally cured by Steiner's loving care. Steiner also taught that the doctor's spiritual interaction with the child is of importance for the doctor's own development. Since Steiner's death, more than a hundred homes for handicapped children have been founded by Anthroposophists.

So at the beginning of 1924—the last full year of his life—Steiner was involved in a bewildering number of activities: education, medicine, agriculture, politics, the Christian community, Eurhythmy and speech training, as well as in lecturing on all aspects of Anthroposophy. He was also engaged in writing his Autobiography, one of his most important books, which appeared in weekly parts in the periodical *The Goetheanum* (edited by Albert Steffen). He was also becoming increasingly preoccupied with problems of karma, and at Dornach in February and March, delivered a series of lectures called 'Esoteric Reflections on Karmic Relationships'. The eight volumes in which these were published are certainly among the most fascinating of Steiner's works, even for readers who are not Anthroposophists. They are far more readable than many of his earlier works, and have a direct, personal tone which conveys his immense charm. They also reveal his enormous knowledge of history, and the sheer breadth of his intelligence. Even for the more-or-less sceptical reader, they are a treasure house of remarkable insights. In April he was in Prague, in May in Paris, and in June in Breslau, where he was a guest on the estate of another philosopher, Count Keyserling, and lectured on agriculture. There followed more lectures in Stuttgart and Dornach, then a trip to Arnhem, in Holland. Then, after more lectures in Dornach, he attended a summer school in Torquay, Devon. But it was clear to his associates that he was beginning to find the pace too much for him; he began to suffer from a stomach ailment that often left him exhausted. Instead of relaxing and taking a holiday, he worked harder than ever: there were seventy lectures in two and a half weeks during the Torquay trip.

Yet his friends seem to be in agreement that what finally caused Steiner's fatal illness was not the travel and lecturing, but the demands of people, many of them strangers. Steffen has described how, after lectures, there would be long queues of people waiting to talk to him about their personal problems. Nothing can be more exhausting than listening to other people's problems. It seems clear that Steiner's major mistake was to make himself available for hundreds of 'personal consultations' when he was already exhausted from lecturing. And after leaving Torquay, he went on to London and gave still more lectures. When he returned to Dornach in September, he was a dying man. On 28 September 1924, he gave what was to be the first of two lectures on St John and the Mystery of Lazarus—he was still lecturing in the workshop, since work on the new Goetheanum had hardly begun. Members who came to hear the second lecture found it unbelievable that Steiner was unable to deliver it because of illness; they had come to think of him as inexhaustible.

From late September until his death the following March, Steiner was unable to leave his bedroom. He still continued to work—Wachsmuth brought in his correspondence every day, he dictated replies to letters, and he continued to write his Autobiography by hand. The festival at Christmas was the first at which he had not been present; he sent a message saying that he was present in spirit.

He seems to have been unaware that this was the end; he told Marie Steiner (they had married in 1914) that he was improving gradually, and that it was imperative that he should get back to work soon. But his suffering became increasingly intense. Outside, he could hear the sounds coming from the workshop, and the noise of the workmen building the new Goetheanum. Then, towards the end of March 1925, the pain suddenly ceased, and he became peaceful and relaxed. On 30 March he folded his hands over his breast, closed his eyes, and died.

Nine

Postscript: Steiner's Achievement

IT IS easy to see why Anthroposophists regard Steiner as the greatest man of the twentieth century, and are inclined to dismiss the idea that he was anything less than perfect. A man who worked so hard and so unselfishly could not be the charlatan portrayed by his enemies. But for the rest of us, it is rather more difficult to arrive at an impartial judgement. Beyond all doubt he was no confidence trickster, no fake messiah driven by an urge to self-aggrandisement. But when we try to arrive at a balanced assessment of what he *was*, the exercise becomes increasingly frustrating.

The most satisfactory method of approach is to try to grasp the essence of Steiner's achievement. What did he have to say that distinguishes him from all other thinkers of the twentieth century?

The answer lies in that recognition we have discussed at some length in the opening chapter: that the 'spirit world' is actually man's *inner* world. He is saying, in effect: the bird is a creature of the air; the fish is a creature of the water; the worm is a creature of the earth. But man is essentially a *creature of the mind*. His true home is a world inside himself. It is true that we have to live in the external world; but, as we saw in the first chapter, we have to retreat inside ourselves if we are to grasp this outer world.

Most of us find it difficult to 'retreat' very far into that inner world; the external world and its problems keep on dragging us back. Steiner seems to have had an altogether extraordinary capacity for descending into his inner world. And the central assertion of his philosophy is that this inner realm *is* the 'spiritual world', and that once man has learned to enter this realm, he realizes that it is not a mere imaginative reflection of the external world, but a world that possesses its own independent reality.

But how is it possible to *make use* of this insight? Here it is necessary for me to speak from personal experience. I have found that, since I began to immerse myself in the life and ideas of Rudolf Steiner, his 'central assertion' has assumed an increasing importance in my attitude towards my own experience. Most of us find that life is a struggle between our feeling of personal individuality and the overwhelming reality of the world around us. The world seems so much bigger and more important than we are. This feeling increases when we are tired or discouraged; at such times, we feel 'stranded' in the external world, like a jelly fish cast up on the beach by the tide. And when this happens, we experience the profoundly discouraging sensation that the external world is 'all there is'—that it is the only reality.

Yet we *know*, deep down, that this is untrue. We only have to be reminded of that inner world by some smell or taste, or by a line of poetry or a few bars of music, to experience a strange inner flood of warmth and strength, the feeling Proust experienced when he tasted the cake dipped in tea, and which made him write: 'I had ceased to feel mediocre, accidental, mortal . . .'. *A la recherche du Temps perdu*

Proust devoted his enormous novel to exploring the problem: How can this feeling be restored at will? Rudolf Steiner had discovered the answer. His early studies of geometry and science had taught him the 'trick' of withdrawing deep inside himself, until it dawned on him that the inner realm is a world in itself, an 'alternative reality', so to speak. Once he knew this, he took care not to forget it. He devoted a certain amount of time every day to *reminding* himself of this truth.

In effect, Steiner's recognition could be compared to the spray carried around by asthma sufferers to ward off attacks. We are all subject to attacks of 'contingency'. The answer lies in developing the trick of reminding oneself of the existence of that inner realm.

I have found that it is best to do this when I am not actually tired, but merely relaxed, or even slightly bored. Most of us experience a certain boredom, a sense of 'taking for granted', when we are on our way home, because we are looking forward to getting there, and the interval between now and then seems rather tiresome. This, I have found, is an excellent time for practising Steiner's trick of 'withdrawal', of reminding myself that this is *not* 'all there is', but that the entrance to an enormous Aladdin's cave lies just inside the threshold of my mind.

The results of this exercise were more interesting than I expected. I found that I not only ceased to feel 'contingent', but that my powers of endurance seemed to be considerably increased. I have noticed this particularly when walking along a very long beach not far from my home, a beach whose soft sand seems to absorb a great deal of energy. I usually plod along stoically, looking forward to getting back home and pouring myself a glass of wine. But when practising the 'Steiner exercise' (as I came to call it), I was suddenly indifferent to the aching in my legs. *It no longer mattered.*

This led to a further insight which I think is worth mentioning. I suspect that we quite unconsciously increase our fatigue by the mere act of being aware of it. If I am on a long walk, and I begin to feel tired, then the mere recognition that I am tired induces a kind of 'negative feedback'. We all know how easily this can happen when we are feeling thoroughly miserable and discouraged; the sense of discouragement can turn into an avalanche that suddenly overwhelms us. My observations during the 'Steiner exercise' made me aware that, quite unconsciously, we do this all the time, and that merely withdrawing slightly into that 'inner world' breaks the negative circuit and releases strength that was otherwise being allowed to run down a kind of mental drain.

I feel that this provides an important clue to Steiner. Looking at the sheer volume of his work—it must run to nearly a million pages—one receives an impression of a cataract of mental energy. As a writer, I am aware of how much mental energy it takes to write a book. Steiner's mind seems to have been in full flood all the time; it never stopped. In order to form an estimate of that intellectual Niagara, one merely has to look at the 1,600 pages of *Karmic Relationships*, delivered between February and September 1924, and to realize that these were only a fraction of the lectures he delivered in that period. Then glance at any chapter of Wachsmuth's *Life*, and see how many lectures he delivered during an average year. One's first reaction is to say: 'The man never stopped thinking.' But all this is not mere 'thinking'. Thinking is the activity we find so abundantly in Bertrand Russell, or Karl Marx, or Sartre, an activity that demands constant pauses for reflection. It seems obvious that Steiner was carried along by a flood of intuitions. Wachsmuth says repeatedly that when Steiner spoke about some event in history, he seemed to be *seeing* what he was describing.

To call this 'active imagination' sounds slightly derogatory, until one grasps what Jung actually meant by the term. For Jung, the 'psychic world' (i.e. world of the mind) was an independent reality, and it was possible to *travel* there and make the acquaintance of its inhabitants.

One of the best examples of 'active imagination' is the curious ability known as psychometry, which was briefly discussed in the opening chapter. Certain people have the ability to hold an object in their hands and to 'see' images from its past history. In recent decades it has even been found to be a valuable aid to archaeology. A remarkable Polish psychic, Stefan Ossowiecki, was told by a friend about Rudolf Steiner and the 'Akasic records', and decided to make a systematic attempt to 'read' them. In association with Professor Stanislaw Poniatowski, of the University of Warsaw, he conducted a detailed series of experiments on prehistoric objects that again and again revealed incredible accuracy.*

But all good psychometrists freely admit that they can easily be confused by the thoughts and expectations of other people, or by their own. Most psychometrists insist on being told nothing whatever about the object they are about to handle, in case this influences what they 'see'.

The evidence suggests that Steiner was a psychometrist of a very high order—Maeterlinck went straight to the point when he said that Steiner used a 'transcendental psychometry'. Unfortunately, he never undertook a series of controlled experiments, so it is quite impossible for us to know how

*See my *Psychic Detectives*, Chapter 7.

No
T. a
Celtic
centre.

many of his visions of the past were genuine, and how many—like the one at Tintagel—were partly imagination. Even so it is important to recognize that the Tintagel experience was not necessarily pure imagination. The Roman general Artorius *is* associated with Cornwall, as the large number of Arthurian place names testify.* Nothing is more likely than that there was some association between Artorius and the Celtic monastery that occupied the Tintagel site in Arthur's lifetime. But when Wachsmuth says: 'He described to us in living pictures—pointing with his hand to the various parts of the castle—where the hall of the Round Table had once been, the rooms of the king and his knights,' we are justified in assuming that he was being influenced by his literary knowledge of the legend.

Where Steiner's real importance is concerned, all this is irrelevant. Bernard Shaw pointed out that the miracles are irrelevant to the teachings of Jesus. 'To say "You should love your enemies; and to convince you of this I will now proceed to cure this gentleman of a cataract" would have been . . . the proposition of an idiot.' And Shaw quotes Rousseau as saying: 'Get rid of the miracles and the whole world will fall at the feet of Jesus Christ.' He argues that Jesus did his best to keep the miracles quiet because he realized that they would distract attention from what he really had to say. This is undoubtedly why Steiner reserved his lectures on karma and allied 'occult' subjects for a small circle of followers; he knew they would only distract attention from his basic teaching on freedom, on the reality of the 'inner world', on man's immense hidden powers of creativity.

Steiner was not, after all, a man whose claim to attention lay in 'psychic powers' or contact with hidden masters. It lay in the *ideas* that are to be found in his books on Goethe, in *The Philosophy of Freedom*, and in the Autobiography. Steiner claimed that what he was saying in those books was the foundation for his later ideas. Yet the truth is that we may decide to ignore the later ideas, or to study them in a spirit of purely intellectual curiosity, without detracting in any way from our sense of the importance of these early books.

*See, for example, my contribution to *King Arthur Country in Cornwall* (Bossiney Books, 1979).

It has been my own experience that, once Steiner's *basic* ideas are understood, everything else falls into place. Problems only arise if we approach Steiner through the 'esoteric' teachings that he himself tried to limit to intimate friends and convinced Anthroposophists. If we begin with *Cosmic Memory* or *Karmic Relationships*, the result is likely to be confusion followed by scepticism. We want to know *how* he claims to know all these things, and he offers no clue. So it is easy to make the assumption that his 'readings' from the Akashic records are pure invention. If we once conclude that he is dishonest, then it becomes equally plain that the turning point came in 1900, when he decided to swallow the doctrines of Theosophy to gain an audience—rather as a poor man might marry an ugly but wealthy widow. The next step is to feel that a man who could compromise his intellectual honesty to this extent must have been a fraud—or at least a lightweight—from the beginning.

Presumably a person who has arrived at this conclusion would never make the attempt to read the Autobiography or *Goethe's Theory of Knowledge*. And this would be a pity, for these two books, the first and last Steiner wrote, make it immediately clear that this man was far too serious a thinker to be dismissed in this way. It would be possible to construct a whole philosophy upon this single sentence from the Goethe book: 'When one who has a rich mental life sees a thousand things which are nothing to the mentally poor, this shows as clearly as sunlight that the content of reality is only the reflection of the content of our minds, and that we receive from without merely the empty form.'

Take *this* as our starting point, and we begin to see Steiner from a completely different point of view. He was a man who was born into a world dominated by scientific materialism. His objection to this materialism was not merely intellectual, or even egotistical (the feeling 'If the world is wholly material, then *I* can't be very important'). It was the feeling that *man is cut off from his inner powers by this superficial attitude*. This is why Steiner shouted at his friend at the Vienna railway station: 'Please note that you never say "my brain thinks", "my brain sees", "my brain walks" ... The fact is, you are lying when you say "I" ...'. A man who believes that thinking is merely some chemical activity of the brain will never make the effort to create a masterpiece.

The problem is that man is trapped in a vision of himself as a nobody, a nonentity. Gurdjieff would have said that this is because so-called waking consciousness is actually a disguised form of sleep. Steiner would have put it slightly differently, and said that it is a problem of 'forgetfulness'. Human beings have *forgotten* that they are free.

The different diagnoses lead to different remedies. For Gurdjieff, man needs to be shaken awake; he needs an 'alarm clock'. The threat of death, for example, instantly wakes him up. The problem is that the 'robot', the mechanical part of us, tends to do most of our living for us. Gurdjieff's answer was to maintain a high level of self-discipline—for example, incredibly complicated physical movements—that would suppress the robot. But even this is not a permanent solution; consciousness is continually falling asleep again.

Steiner's answer is, by comparison, far more optimistic. If man has forgotten that he is free, his problem is simply to remind himself. Like Faust, he needs to remember that

> The spirit world is never closed;
> Your heart is dead, your senses sleep . . .

To grasp the essence of Steiner, we only need to re-read that opening scene in *Faust*, where the overworked scholar, depressed and exhausted, feels tempted to commit suicide. But as he raises the poison to his lips, the Easter Bells begin to ring, bringing back a flood of memories of childhood—the 'Proust effect'. And Faust dissolves into tears of happiness, *remembering* that life is infinitely complex and infinitely exciting.

Hermann Hesse captured the same vision in his own version of *Faust*, the novel *Steppenwolf*. The hero is another bored scholar who suspects that life is a malicious joke. He broods on suicide. Then, as he sits in a tavern, eating his evening meal with a glass of Moselle, he experiences pure delight: 'A refreshing laughter rose in me . . . It soared aloft like a soap bubble . . . and then softly burst . . . The golden trail was blazed, and I was reminded of the eternal, and of Mozart and the stars . . .'.

It is as if the doorway to an *inner* Aladdin's cave has swung open. He realizes that human beings possess a *sense of reality*, a certain faculty that gives us access to reality. (I have elsewhere called this 'Faculty X'.)

We can see that the real problem of Faust and Steppenwolf is that they have not only allowed themselves to forget this 'other' reality—Mozart and the stars—but that they have gone to the other extreme, and constructed a mental vision that is based on the feeling that life is stupid and futile.

How can they combat this negative insight? Gurdjieff would say: by constructing elaborate 'alarm clocks' and accepting 'intentional suffering'. But there is obviously a more straightforward solution. If I really *want* to remember something, then I can do so. I can sit and think about Faust and Proust and Steppenwolf, until my gloom has evaporated and I realize that the 'negative insight' is a mixture of muddle-headedness and self-pity. If I do this often enough, I shall gradually cease to become subject to apathy and discouragement. I shall realize that the *objective facts* of human existence justify immense optimism, and that the main thing that prevents us from grasping this is simply childishness, a failure to grow up.

There was another respect in which Steiner was more optimistic than Gurdjieff. Gurdjieff said that man is deluded to believe he has an 'essential ego', a real 'I'. The truth, said Gurdjieff, is that man has hundreds of 'I's', and they keep replacing one another with bewildering rapidity, so man is like a country that has never known a stable government. Steiner would agree that there is an element of truth in this, but he would argue that it is not a fundamental problem. According to Steiner, the existence of an 'I' is precisely what distinguishes man from the lower animals. We might compare a dog or cat to a group of travelling musicians who wander through the streets playing more or less in unison; but man is an orchestra with a conductor. The travelling players make a perfectly good job of 'Home, sweet home'. But only the orchestra can do justice to Beethoven's ninth symphony.

The problem, according to Steiner, is that man continues to behave as if he were a group of travelling musicians; he never attempts anything more ambitious than 'Home, sweet home'.

Why? Because the conductor is sitting among the orchestra, smoking a cigarette, unaware that he *is* the conductor. It is only in certain moments of excitement or crisis that he remembers who he is, and seizes the baton. Then the orchestra responds by playing magnificently. If he made them practise every day, the results would clearly be superb.

Again, we can see that it is a problem of forgetfulness rather than 'sleep'. If the conductor makes a habit of rehearsing twice a day, the problem will vanish.

Steiner goes further than this—and this is his own central contribution to modern thought. He states that once we have made a habit of remembering Mozart and the stars, we shall find ourselves developing powers of 'spiritual vision'. We shall never again feel ourselves to be helpless victims of the external world. At present, man is subject to misery, distress, and mental strain because he keeps drifting into a kind of short-sightedness and forgetfulness. Any serious crisis makes him *see* how lucky he is, and that the problems that normally oppress him are sheer trivialities. He merely has to learn to *grasp* this so he will never forget it. And, as we all know, it is quite easy to do this if you tell yourself it really matters. When that is accomplished, says Steiner, we shall not only cease to be subject to anxiety and fatigue, but will find ourselves standing on the threshold of a new spiritual world, and developing powers that we never even suspected we possessed.

Steiner claims that his own practice of 'remembering'—of meditating upon these basic truths—had the result of developing his own spiritual powers, including the power of 'vision' possessed by such men as Boehme, Swedenborg, and Blake. These visions, it must be emphasized, were *inward* occurrences. Swedenborg did not imagine he saw angels in the streets of Stockholm; he had to withdraw into a peculiar inner state in order to become aware of them. Steiner admits that this faculty is a form of imagination, but immediately points out that the general usage of the word 'imagination' gives only the faintest idea of what he means. We might say that, in most of us, the faculty of imagination is like the picture on some worn out black-and-white television set, continually flickering and distorting and vanishing; by comparison, Steiner's imagination was like a new colour television with a large screen. And, according to Steiner, he *used* this faculty to amplify his visions of 'spiritual reality'.

We are now in a position to grasp the real tragedy of Rudolf Steiner. He was one of the greatest men of the twentieth century, and it would be impossible to exaggerate the importance of what he had to say. But in order to make himself heard ('Must I remain silent?') he had to take the dangerous step of becoming a preacher and a 'spiritual leader'. This is like hiring a carriage with a dozen powerful and uncontrollable horses. Even a politician finds it difficult to stop them from galloping around in circles. A 'spiritual leader' is lucky if he can prevent them from taking him in the opposite direction from the one he wants to go in.

Shaw expressed the problem with considerable insight in *The Perfect Wagnerite*. Wotan, the ruler of the gods, symbolizes pure idealism. But in order to translate his ideals into action, he has to form an alliance with the forces of the law, and to seal the bargain, he has to sacrifice one of his eyes. The man of pure genius always has to compromise when he wants to put his ideals into action.

Steiner's great compromise was to join the Theosophical Society. He can hardly be blamed for this. He had been an obscure academic, pathetically grateful when a group of working men offered him eight marks for a course of lectures. Then, suddenly, he had an appreciative audience who hung on every word he said. Within a mere decade, his teachings had reached remote corners of the world. The Goetheanum rose on its hilltop in Dornach, a symbol of the ultimate triumph of the spirit. Steiner did what he had to do, and it would be pointless to find fault with him.

Yet the Goetheanum is also the symbol of everything that stands between Steiner and his potential modern audience. It is the visible church of Anthroposophy, and its scriptures include *Cosmic Memory*, *Karmic Relationships*, *Christianity as Mystical Fact*, *Rosicrucian Esotericism*, *The Reappearance of Christ in the Etheric*, and a hundred or so other volumes with confusing titles and bewildering contents. For the Anthroposophist—and even for the open-minded sceptic—they are full of important insights. But their sheer quantity constitutes an enormous obstacle between Steiner and the intelligent reader. Steiner's incredible industry was self-defeating. The mountain of titles, the avalanche of ideas, obscures the clarity and simplicity of his basic insight.

Nevertheless, for the reader who declines to be discouraged, the rewards can be enormous. Once the basic insight has been grasped, we can begin to understand the source of those tremendous mental energies, and the sheer breadth of Steiner's vision. It hardly matters that there is a great deal that we may find unacceptable, or even repellent. What is so absorbing is to be in contact with a mind that was capable of this astonishing range of inner experience.

Steiner was a man who had discovered an important secret; his books are fascinating because they contain continual glimpses of this secret. We may read them critically, wondering where Steiner was 'amplifying' genuine intuitions, and where he was amplifying his own dreams and imaginings. We may even conclude that Swedenborg, Blake, and Madame Blavatsky had all developed the same power of amplification, and that Steiner's visions of angelic hierarchies are no truer than Swedenborg's visions of heaven and hell, Blake's visions of the daughters of Albion, or Madame Blavatsky's visions of the giants of Atlantis. But all that is beside the point. The real point is that this faculty of amplification is our human birthright, and that anyone who can grasp this can learn to pass through that door to the inner universe as easily as he could stroll through the entrance of the British Museum.

Bibliography

BOOKS ON RUDOLF STEINER

Rudolf Steiner: Recollections by Some of his Pupils (Golden Blade, 1958).

Ahern, Geoffrey, *Sun at Midnight. Rudolf Steiner and the Western Esoteric Tradition* (Aquarian Press, Wellingborough, Northamptonshire, 1984).

Clark, Laurence, *Coming to Terms with Rudolf Steiner* (Veracity Ventures, Hertfordshire, 1971).

Davy, John, *Work Arising From The Life of Rudolf Steiner* (Rudolf Steiner Press, London, 1975).

Easton, S. C., *Man and World in the Light of Anthroposophy* (The Anthroposophic Press, New York, 1975).

——, *Rudolf Steiner, Herald of a New Epoch* (The Anthroposophic Press, New York, 1980).

Edmunds, Francis, *Rudolf Steiner's Gift to Education – The Waldorf Schools* (Rudolf Steiner Press, London, 1975).

——, *Anthroposophy. A Way of Life* (Carnant Books, East Sussex, 1982).

Freeman, Arnold, *Meditation Under the Guidance of Rudolf Steiner* (The Sheffield Educational Settlement, Sheffield, 1957).

Grohmann, Gerbert, *The Plant* (Rudolf Steiner, London, 1974).

Harwood, A. C., *The Recovery of Man in Childhood* (The Anthroposophic Press, New York, 1958).

Hemleben, Johannes, *Rudolf Steiner. A Documentary Biography* (Henry Goulden Limited, Sussex, 1975).

Mayer, Gladys, *Behind the Veils of Death and Sleep* (New Knowledge Books, East Grinstead, Sussex).

Nesfield-Cookson, Bernard, *Rudolf Steiner's Vision of Love* (Aquarian Press, Wellingborough, Northamptonshire, 1983).

Palmer, Otto, *Rudolf Steiner on his book The Philosophy of Freedom* (The Anthroposophic Press, New York, 1975).

Rittelmeyer, Friedrich, *Rudolf Steiner Enters my Life* (Floris Books, Edinburgh, 1982).

Savitch, Marie, *Marie Steiner-von Sivers* (Rudolf Steiner Press, London, 1967).

Shepherd, A. P., *A Scientist of the Invisible* (Floris Classics, Edinburgh, 1983).
Steffen, Albert, *Meetings with Rudolf Steiner* (Verlag Für Schöne Wissenschaften, Switzerland, 1961).
Wachsmuth, Gunter, *The Life and Work of Rudolf Steiner* (Whittier Books, New York, 1955).

SELECTED LIST OF BOOKS BY RUDOLF STEINER

Ancient Myths. Their Meaning and Connection with Evolution (Steiner Book Centre, Canada, 1971).
Atlantis and Lemuria (Anthroposophical Publishing Co., London, 1923).
An Autobiography (Rudolf Steiner Publications, 1977).
Between Death and Rebirth (Rudolf Steiner Press, London, 1975).
The Case for Anthroposophy (Rudolf Steiner Press, London, 1970).
Christianity as Mystical Fact (Rudolf Steiner Publishing Co., London, 1948).
Cosmic Memory (Rudolf Steiner Publications, New York, 1959).
The Dead Are With Us [lecture, 10 February 1918] (Rudolf Steiner Press, 1964).
Descriptive Sketches of the Spiritual World (Anthroposophical Publishing Co., London, 1928).
The Four Mystery Plays (Rudolf Steiner Press, London, 1982).
Goethe's Secret Revelation, and The Riddle in Faust (Rudolf Steiner Press, 1932).
Karmic Relationships. Esoteric Studies, Volumes I–VIII (Rudolf Steiner Press, London, 1981).
Knowledge of the Higher Worlds (Rudolf Steiner Publishing Co., London, 1937).
Mystery Knowledge and Mystery Centres (Rudolf Steiner Press, London, 1973).
Friedrich Nietzsche (Rudolf Steiner Publications, Inc., New Jersey, USA, 1960).
The Occult Movement in the Nineteenth Century (Rudolf Steiner Press, London, 1973).
The Occult Significance of the Bhagavad Gita (Anthroposophic Press Inc., New York, 1968).
Occult Signs and Symbols (Anthroposophic Press, Inc., New York, 1972).
An Outline of Occult Science (Theosophical Publishing Society, London, 1914; Rand McNally & Co., New York, 1914).
The Philosophy of Freedom (Rudolf Steiner Press, London, 1964).
Reincarnation and Immortality (Rudolf Steiner Publications, New York, 1970).

The Riddles of Philosophy (The Anthroposophic Press, New York, 1973).

A Road to Self-Knowledge and The Threshold of the Spiritual World (Rudolf Steiner Press, London, 1975).

Rosicrucian Esotericism (The Anthroposophic Press, New York, 1978).

Study of Man (Rudolf Steiner Press, London, 1966).

A Theory of Knowledge (The Anthroposophic Press, New York, 1968).

Theosophy (Kegan Paul, Trench, Trübner & Co., Ltd., London, 1910).

World Economy (Rudolf Steiner Press, London, 1972).

World History in the Light of Anthroposophy (Rudolf Steiner Press, London, 1950).

Index